## Praise for *Building Conflict Competent Teams*

"This book takes conflict competence to a whole new level—beyond enhancing individual skills to the ever more important team setting. Full of informative, helpful tools, tips, and guidance, teams and team leaders will learn how to transform conflict into opportunity and increase their 'teamness.' Through meaningful stories and examples, exercises, and specific techniques, the reader learns how to manage emotion, communicate more effectively, and overcome obstacles to resolving conflict in team settings."

—Kathy Bryan, president and CEO, International Institute for Conflict Prevention & Resolution

"In today's fast-paced lifestyle and culture, leaders and organizations increasingly face challenges and obstacles created by internal team conflict. Runde and Flanagan teach us that not all team conflicts are bad, and those constructive team conflicts, if managed and integrated properly, can lead to dynamic improvements in team creativity and production. Now, in *Building Conflict Competent Teams*, you can learn the principles that will help you lead your team to the top of its game."

—Ben J. Hayes, president, New York–Penn League

"A very practical, easily understood approach to team conflict management. Runde and Flanagan provide real-life, easy-to-relate-to examples and actionable 'how to's' with useful application tools."

—William K. Rusak, executive vice president, human resources, Corrections Corporation of America

# Building Conflict Competent Teams

Craig E. Runde

Tim A. Flanagan

JOSSEY-BASS
A Wiley Imprint
www.josseybass.com

Center for
Creative
Leadership
NORTH AMERICA  EUROPE  ASIA
www.ccl.org

Published by Jossey-Bass
A Wiley Imprint
989 Market Street, San Francisco, CA 94103-1741—www.josseybass.com

Readers should be aware that Internet Web sites offered as citations and/or sources for further
information may have changed or disappeared between the time this was written and when
it is read.

Jossey-Bass books and products are available through most bookstores. To contact Jossey-Bass
directly call our Customer Care Department within the U.S. at 800-956-7739, outside the U.S.
at 317-572-3986, or fax 317-572-4002.

Jossey-Bass also publishes its books in a variety of electronic formats. Some content that appears
in print may not be available in electronic books.

**Library of Congress Cataloging-in-Publication Data**

Runde, Craig E.
    Building conflict competent teams / Craig E. Runde, Tim A. Flanagan.—1st ed.
        p.   cm.
    Includes bibliographical references and index.
    ISBN 978-0-470-18947-4 (cloth)
        1. Teams in the workplace—Management.   2. Interpersonal conflict.   3. Conflict
management.   I. Flanagan, Tim A.   II. Title.
    HD66.R86   2008
    658.4'022—dc22

                                                                          2008004730

Printed in the United States of America
FIRST EDITION
HB Printing          10 9 8 7 6 5 4 3 2 1

A Joint Publication of
The Jossey-Bass
Business & Management Series
and
The Center for Creative Leadership

# Contents

To the "small town girl and the lucky Marine,"
my parents, Jeanne and Pat Flanagan, who provided
the climate I needed early in life. And to Harriet and
Charles McIntire, the parents of my wife, Mac,
who provides all I need now.

To my loving parents, Gerry and Barney Runde, and
my wonderful wife Kathy's parents, Patricia and John Fenn.
They have shown me that a sense of humor can
help through life's conflicts.

# Preface

The idea for this book developed from a conversation with our editor, Kathe Sweeney. We were exploring various options for a follow-up to our first book, *Becoming a Conflict Competent Leader*. After discussing a number of ideas and alternatives, Kathe suggested looking at teams and conflict. The moment she said this, we all knew it was the right idea.

Over the years, we have worked with numerous teams that have struggled with conflict. Many have endured the dysfunctions that come from poorly managed conflict. We have observed strained interactions, dwindling communication, the absence of information sharing, and stalled initiative. We have witnessed previously collaborative, creative, vibrant teams grow distressed and uncertain about how to recover. We have seen relationships and productivity suffer.

We have also personally experienced conflict in teams. Conflict may be inevitable, but it does not have to lead to poor results and damaged relationships. It is possible for teams to work through conflict confidently, although this can be challenging at times. In fact, we believe that conflict handled effectively can inspire creative solutions to problems, provide the foundation for stronger relationships, and result in confident, more capable, and highly productive teams.

Our goal in this book is to help teams discover how to get the best out of conflict while navigating through the obstacles, discomfort, and challenges it can bring. We examine the nature of conflict in teams, as well as the emotional, behavioral, and

process approaches you can use to help your team become conflict competent.

## Outline of the Book

This book begins with a real story about a team that faced a
number of uphill challenges and difficult conflicts. It shows that
conflict can bring both positive and negative results, depending on how a team addresses it. This is followed in Chapter Two
with a look at when and how conflict emerges in teams. You will
see why conflict is a regular feature of team life and why it is so
difficult for teams to manage effectively. Understanding the reasons that conflict is challenging provides hints about what teams
need to do to get the best out of it.

Chapters Three and Four, the heart of the book, examine
how teams can rise to the challenges of conflict. In Chapter
Three, we analyze what teams must do to create an effective
climate for dealing with conflict. Without such a climate, team
members will not have sufficient trust and emotional control
to be able to talk with one another openly and honestly when
conflicts arise. Without openness and honesty, the true nature
of issues cannot be explored, and conflicts will fester as people
assume the worst about others' intentions.

Chapter Four introduces and explores specific constructive
communication behaviors that enable teammates to discuss
issues in ways that lead to satisfying resolutions instead of contentious finger-pointing. While creating the right climate is a necessary step, constructive behavioral responses produce the interactive
foundation on which teams can build to achieve breakthroughs.
The consistent use of constructive behaviors among team members helps keep the climate positive for future interactions.
Chapters Three and Four also provide team leaders with suggestions about ways in which they can help their team improve its
climate and communications.

In Chapter Five we look at techniques to use when, despite
having the right climate and using constructive communications,

conflicts present tough challenges. These techniques can help teams get things back on track when conflicts have stalled productivity, damaged relationships, or stifled creativity. These tools can help teams reestablish the climate and communication necessary to fuel continued development and success.

Changes in technology and organizational structures are creating new kinds of teams. In Chapter Six we examine how virtual teams can address conflict given the limitations associated with technology-mediated communications. These teams face many of the same challenges as teams that meet face-to-face, but they have to do so with different kinds of communication approaches. We also look at teams made up of members from different cultures because cultural differences can lead to conflicts and complicate the process of resolving them.

In the final chapter we provide some practical tools to help you get your team started on the road to conflict competence by assessing how well your team currently manages conflict. In addition, we provide some specific suggestions to improve the conflict climate in your team, as well as your ability to communicate constructively. We have also included a Resources section at the end of the book listing organizations that provide services that can be helpful to teams addressing conflict.

## Acknowledgments

We would not have been able to write this book without the help and support of a great many people. First, we acknowledge Kathe Sweeney, Brian Grimm, Maria Meneses, Mary Garrett, and the extraordinary team at Jossey-Bass who make a project like this possible.

We also thank James Deegan, vice president and dean at Eckerd College. Jim, our boss, has consistently supported our writing, and his encouragement has meant a great deal to us. We also thank our colleagues at the Leadership Development Institute at Eckerd College, who have provided feedback and advice along the way.

We received suggestions, assistance, and stories from friends and colleagues, team members and team leaders, executives and experts. The list includes Matt Jones, Brad Williams, Joe Tomaselli, Jay Feaster, Jay Preble, Gary Shelton, Michael Kossler, Ben Hayes, Sharon Grady, Joe Carella, Joanne McCree, Wayne Jones, Maggie Dunn, Dennis M. Dennis, Susan Gunn, Amanda Pace, Sherod Miller, Michael Rawlings, Maya Hu-Chan, Ken Bradt, Robert Prescott, Peter Maida, Kim Kanaga, Sue Raub, Ethan Mayefsky, Laurie Kelly, Judy Ringer, Ann Mooney, Patricia Holahan, Allen Amason, Kathy Jehn, Astrid Homan, and Lindred Greer.

We spent many hours discussing our progress, or lack thereof, in some of our favorite dining establishments in St. Petersburg. Thanks to the owners and staff of The Chattaway, Skyway Jack's, Tangelo's Grill, Spartan, and Munches for patiently allowing us to commandeer tables for more than just a meal.

Finally, we thank our families for putting up with us during the long stretches when we were more focused on the book than our loved ones. Our wonderful wives, Mac and Kathy, have given us moral support throughout the process and unparalleled practical assistance in proofing the copy. Our children have been pillars of support as well. Tim is grateful for the many brilliant suggestions and observations from Lindsay and Kyle. Craig thanks his son, Matthew, for his substantial help with research and transcription. Both of us thank Matthew for creating the figures in the book.

Finally, we thank the teams and team members who have allowed us into their worlds. Their willingness to share the reality of their experiences with us, their pain and frustration, their struggles and dismay, their joy and elation, their commitment and satisfaction, provided true inspiration. Most of all, this book is for you.

*St. Petersburg, Florida*                                    Tim A. Flanagan
*April 2008*                                                 Craig E. Runde

# Building Conflict
# Competent Teams

# 1

# A TEAM IN CONFLICT

In the middle of difficulty lies opportunity.

*—Albert Einstein*

We love a good story. You know the kind we're talking about. Our favorite stories share common themes of underdogs thrust into pivotal roles, good people persevering, a few unexpected twists, and ultimately a celebration of good triumphing over evil. The very best ones get passed on from generation to generation and beg to be retold time and again.

We hope the story we're about to tell shares these characteristics. At the very least, we hope it is one you will feel good about sharing with others. Oh, one more thing: this story is absolutely true. We'll reveal the identity of this rather amazing real-life tale a few pages from now. Until then, take note of the conflicts contained in the storyline. Look for the impact of each conflict and how these conflicts were addressed. See if you can find value in how the conflicts were handled. We also hope you find yourself guessing at the identity of the organization. So don't look ahead. Just sit back, relax, and enjoy.

## The Organization

The organization had long aspired to be thought of as world class in a highly competitive industry. Over the years, it had gained a reputation for being long on potential, but it had failed to reach and maintain the peak level of performance and results for which it was founded. Only once in its sixty-year history had the organization been considered truly one of the best in its class.

This achievement was short-lived, considered a fluke, and never again attained.

The organization had many characteristics that were the envy of its competitors. Its facilities and offices were top notch. State-of-the-art equipment and tools were in place. The investment in education and training of personnel was second to none. The organization's board and stakeholders were generous with their support. Executive leaders and content experts were among the most experienced and talented in the world. Their product was truly a source of pride for all associates. And consumers were willing, even eager, to embrace the organization and its product. Despite all these stellar characteristics, the organization somehow seemed to wallow through its existence, never producing the kind of results for which it seemed so capable. Potential evolved into frustration. Eventually frustration led to a changing of the leadership.

## The Search

As the board searched for the right executive to take over the reins, the search committee found the organization to be a tougher sell than they had anticipated. The board was committed to recruiting the very best leader available. The compensation package was certainly worthy of a world-class leader, and the challenge of leading this well-known but underachieving organization seemed likely to spur the interest of the very best of the best. As time passed, the search committee found itself in the unlikely position of seeing its top candidate bow out of the running. Left with but a few solid candidates, the board decided to offer the top position to a man who was well known in the field and had significant experience and a compelling record of success, but he had never presided over an organization of this size and significance. He was also known for his intense, driving, even demanding personality. He demonstrated this characteristic during his final interview when he made two rather unique requests of the search committee and the board. First, he suggested a radical new method of operations. Second, he wanted their support for embarking on a nationwide search for talented employees. And he wanted to personally spearhead the search and the subsequent orientation and training of these new associates. In fact, without these accommodations, he said he would not consider accepting the position if offered.

The search committee pondered their decision. The risks were weighed, résumés reviewed, and candidates discussed. In the end, the committee decided to offer their prized top leadership role to this experienced and admittedly demanding man, whom we'll call Bert. Amid appropriate fanfare, he was introduced as the organization's best hope for finally fulfilling its promise.

## Finding New Talent

Bert was thrilled with the opportunity and poured himself into his new role. True to form, he set out to find the most highly talented staff available. Because he had years of experience in the industry, he knew exactly where to look. Many of those he targeted for recruitment were well known to him from past industry competition and conferences. He knew that to find the most talented people, he would have to recruit from a number of different organizations, some of them fierce competitors. Within a few weeks, he contacted scores of experts and invited them for interviews and testing. And with the board's blessing, he hired a "lieutenant," whom we'll call Pat, to assist him in his recruiting, selection, and training efforts.

Over a fairly short period of a time, Bert and Pat whittled the field of potential new associates down to about two dozen. Some of the candidates withdrew their candidacy in reaction to Bert's methods and approach. Others privately wondered whether they would want to work for a man seemingly so focused and intense. Some questioned the wisdom of recruiting people who had openly, sometimes brazenly, competed with one another in the past. In addition, the business practices and standards of these competing organizations were often markedly different. The potential for conflict among the new staff seemed incredibly high. Those who ultimately accepted the offer to become new members of the organization knew that they faced a steep challenge.

## Conflicting Perspectives

Bert created an orientation and training process designed to leverage the best attributes of his newly hired team. He had already drawn criticism over his selections of personnel; some of the board members, in fact, openly questioned his judgment. Bert's response was that each person had been selected to fill a specific role on the team. He admitted that not each person was the top expert in his field. Rather, he likened each new person to a piece of a larger puzzle. Each piece needed to fit perfectly. In his quest for that perfect fit, he demanded thoroughness of preparation and an unrelenting focus on fundamental knowledge and skills. His newly hired charges sometimes grew weary of Bert's passion and tireless drive to craft the members into a single unit. He expected his staff to embrace his vision and pursue it with conviction. Unfortunately, his expectations were not always met.

To make matters worse, a number of the new associates carried baggage from previous relationships and interactions with one another. Several members were absolutely incensed that some of their new colleagues had been competitors, even enemies, in their previous work. One example of the bad blood among the group involved a prestigious industry award that had been bestowed on a company from Minnesota. Several members of that organization were now among Bert's new recruits. As luck would have it, several members of the second-place company for that award were also new members of Bert's organization.

The award had been hotly contested, and the winners were accused (by the second-place organization) of unethical practices that led directly to the award. Not surprisingly, the bitterness of that event carried over into the new organization and contributed to the rift among team members. Moreover, some of the new associates' best friends had been rejected for positions in the firm in favor of those with whom they had competed in the past. It seemed virtually impossible to fathom that this group would be able to work together as associates, somehow putting aside past differences.

Finally, there were moments when Bert and Pat failed to see eye-to-eye. As Bert pushed his troops to stretch beyond their previous limits, Pat sometimes questioned his tactics. Team members complained to Pat about Bert's demanding standards and practices. But Pat absolutely believed in Bert's expertise and supported the notion that the new team members had to work as one in order to be successful. Nevertheless, he occasionally wondered if Bert's tactics were aligned with their ultimate mission and goals. Pat found himself yielding to Bert's decisions often without sharing his thoughts or perspectives.

As Bert pushed his agenda, patience and restraint among the workers wore thin. Tempers flared. Associates avoided one another. Teammates talked behind each other's backs. There were even a few reports of physical altercations. In addition, Pat privately wondered if Bert's passion was interfering with his decision making. Bert's grand design appeared to be in jeopardy. The board members who had hired him just a few months earlier began having doubts. Could their ultimate goal sink any further from realization?

## Turning Points

As the weeks wore on, training sessions, exercises, and simulations gave way to real business engagements. Along the way, a number of events signaled that the organization was beginning to come together. In one case, several associates took it on themselves to acknowledge and confront poor behaviors associated with the bad history among some of their teammates. This led to constructive discussions about the past and agreements to move forward. Another example involved the relationship between Bert and Pat. Bert began to more openly seek Pat's perspective regarding his approach and tactics. Pat confided that he questioned some of them. They talked and worked through their differences while forging an even more respectful partnership. In another case, near the end of one particularly demanding training session, one associate spoke passionately about the need for the group to work as one. This associate was later selected to become one of a few designated team leaders. These examples, and many similar others, showed a resolve to work through the differences, disagreements, and discord. But none demonstrated this organization's ability to deal with conflict better than the following.

Bert believed in training. He offered scores of opportunities for the new associates to participate in exercises and simulations to sharpen their skills, develop relationships, and establish the culture of the now restructured organization. Near the end of the orientation and training period, Bert brought in a new associate. This person had worked for Bert in the past and was a recognized expert and top performer. He was undeniably a great potential resource and asset for the team. Nevertheless, many associates objected to the introduction of a new teammate at this stage of the organization's development. Several sought a meeting with Bert to discuss their disapproval and disappointment over the introduction of the new associate. They described how the current members had formed a bond and that introducing a new member now could interfere with their team development. During their dialogue, Bert asked if the current team was the best it could be. The associates answered that it might not yet be, but that the trust they had developed was the foundation on which the organization could successfully continue to build in its quest of their ultimate goal. Bert's eyes twinkled as he agreed not to upset the delicate balance that had been forged and subsequently released the new associate. The organization had come full circle.

## Success

The new company took off. In the span of just a few days, its success was documented in the headlines of newspapers and as the lead story on newscasts. The team effort displayed drew praise from pundits far and wide. A sense of wonder and admiration grew from around the country, even the rest of the world. The years of frustration seemed to melt away like icicles glinting and dripping in the warm spring sunshine. The conflicts of the past few months paled in comparison to the sweet taste of victory and achievement. Bert's vision, his dream, and the dream of the entire organization had been realized. "Do you believe in miracles? . . . Yes!!" screamed broadcaster Al Michaels as he described the final seconds of the improbable victory on national television. The 1980 U.S. Olympic Hockey Team had defeated the highly favored Soviet Union team in the first game of the medal round. They went on to win the gold medal.

## Upon Further Review

The gold medal win of the 1980 U.S. Olympic Hockey Team is arguably one of the biggest underdog achievements of all time. Its victory over the Soviet team, which had won over forty-five games in a row at the time, was dubbed the "Miracle on Ice." It is the story of teammates achieving through hard work and perseverance. It is the story of a leader (Bert is Herb Brooks) who provided focus, vision, and a belief in the team. It's the story of a team overcoming incredible odds, barriers, and limitations as they established a climate of trust and collaboration. It is the story of an assistant coach (Pat is Craig Patrick) who often provided encouragement and support to team members. And it's a story that illustrates how a team handled conflict in ways that enabled it to succeed beyond its wildest dreams.

## Ingredients for Conflict Competence

I (Tim) was a young man in graduate school in 1980. I remember watching the astonishing victory of the U.S. Hockey Team over the Soviet Union with some friends in my tiny apartment in Columbus, Ohio. We whooped our approval, toasted the players (who were roughly our age), and reveled in amazement. But I had no idea of the true depth of this team's achievement. At the time, I viewed it like virtually every other sports fan did: the incredible story of a bunch of relatively unknown kids defeating the best hockey team in the world. Today it's remembered as one of the biggest upsets in modern team sports history. I also submit that it is a wonderful example of a conflict competent team. Let's review several key characteristics of the 1980 U.S. Olympic Hockey Team that illustrate what it takes to achieve conflict competence as a team.

First, consider the climate the team was able to create in a relatively short period of time. Coach Brooks was clear in his vision of creating a new style of play necessary to compete at the highest level. He was equally clear that this new style would emphasize speed and conditioning. He spoke most often, however, about the team chemistry that would be necessary to implement the new style of play. Technique, skill, and ability alone could not produce the desired results; something more intangible was critical. Team chemistry, the climate, and the quality of the interactions between and among players had to be just right.

The coaches and players came together over a span of mere months. During this time, they established relationships resulting not only in the ability to read one another's moves on the ice but bonds that have lasted a lifetime. Their mission was admittedly unique: it required that team members didn't just play hockey together; they became a family that literally worked, traveled, and lived together. Certainly most of the people reading this book are members of teams that work long, demanding hours but stop somewhere short of living together. Nevertheless, establishing the right climate is critical for handling conflict. Teams must develop trust, and team members must feel safe. Emotions must be handled with care. These essential ingredients of the right climate—trust, safety, and emotional intelligence—are necessary for building conflict competent teams.

Next consider the level of collaboration among the team-mates. For the casual fan watching the games, the collaborative effort could be easily taken for granted. Most of us expect athletic teams, especially those performing at high levels, to be models of "teamness." One of the defining characteristics of this team was the way the players came together and worked as a single unit during their amazing run at the Olympic Games. Their collaborative effort was based on a number of key factors. The team clearly had a specific game plan crafted by the coach, Herb Brooks. Moreover, the players embraced the plan, and everyone understood it. Everyone knew their specific role and accepted responsibility for fulfilling that role. Players held each other accountable. In the early stages of the team's development, Coach Brooks was much more involved in holding team members accountable. As the team evolved, the players held one another accountable. Expectations were clear, and team members were committed to them. These factors led to a mutual accountability among the players that fed their collaborative efforts.

One way to describe the team's method of working together is "complete collaboration." A similar but slightly more expansive term that we will use throughout the book is *behavioral integration*. The highest levels of behavioral integration are characterized by mutual accountability, collaboration, collective decision making, and shared expectations. The 1980 U.S. Hockey Team demonstrated each of these at virtually every juncture of their development. (Collective decision making is probably the least obvious of these characteristics. It was most evident in the later stages of development and was clearest during games and when the team traveled together. However, one of the best examples of collective decision making was illustrated when team members decided to confront Coach Brooks about the potential addition of a new player late in the training program.)

Finally, consider the quality of communication among team members. It's no secret that the team members had to overcome some significant emotional challenges and barriers as they developed into a high-performing team. Stories abound regarding the friction among players who had played for opposing college teams. In fact, a number of players from the University of Minnesota and Boston University had been involved in one of the nastiest college hockey brawls in memory during the 1976 NCAA tournament (Coffey, 2005). Not surprisingly, there was no love lost among these strange bedfellows. As the team experienced training camp together, players had to interact. In fact, the team concept that Coach Brooks demanded made it impossible not to interact.

A shining example of high-quality communication is illustrated by the way teammates resolved long-standing feuds. Teammates sometimes served as mediators for those who were at odds. Coach Patrick stepped in to help teammates communicate through their difficulties. At other times, teammates simply agreed to talk things out among themselves. Addressing difficulties is but one circumstance requiring productive communication. The most conflict competent teams not only address their difficulties effectively, they communicate constructively nearly all the time (no team is perfect). It is imperative that team members communicate frequently with clarity and care. We'll refer to this characteristic throughout the book as *constructive communication*.

In the movie *Miracle*, the silver screen depiction of the 1980 team, one of the most dramatic scenes depicts the aftermath of a lackluster performance during an exhibition game several months prior to the start of the Olympics. The game ended in a tie. During the game Coach Brooks noticed poor communication among his players and a lack of accountability and collaboration. To his great dismay, he saw evidence that the team chemistry had eroded.

After the postgame handshake with the opposing team, he ordered his team to stay on the ice. He expressed his disappointment with the team's effort and lack of commitment to its principles. In an act of legendary proportion, he challenged his players to reach a higher level and began pushing the team through line drills. These drills are essentially wind sprints on skates where players line up at one end of the rink and then skate back and forth between the lines on the ice at top speed. It's an exhausting exercise designed to build stamina. In this case, though, stamina was not Coach Brooks's main goal. Bear in mind these sprints were taking place after the completion of a full game when players were already tired. During brief breaks between sprints, the story portrays Coach Brooks asking loudly of players, "Who do you play for?" In turn, players responded with "Boston University," or "University of Minnesota," or " Bowling Green," and the others. The sprints continued until Mike Eruzione, later named captain, shouted, "I play for the United States of America!" Upon hearing Eruzione's exclamation, Coach Brooks ended the drills. The point was clear. The team had reached a crossroads, a turning point of sorts. The players identified themselves as a single unit signified by a single name. Team identity, team chemistry, teamness—whatever you call it, this dramatization points out that the most conflict competent teams identify themselves first and foremost as a team, not as a loose group of individuals.

## A Great But Not Perfect Example

As we studied the story of the 1980 U.S. Olympic Hockey team, we found some methods and characteristics that we are not suggesting as examples of exemplary team effectiveness.

For instance, not all of Coach Brooks's approaches demonstrated great relationship building. In fact, most accounts suggest that he purposely distanced himself from the players and left relationship building to Craig Patrick, his assistant coach. And not every interaction between and among players set the standard for effective communication or collaboration. The players had plenty of differences.

This team had its warts, as all teams do. Team members sometimes caused conflicts and perpetuated them. The coach was often the target of the players' disdain. The point is, that as conflicts were encountered, this team found effective ways to deal with them. In many cases, conflicts formed the bedrock for building stronger intra-team relationships and collaboration. Conflicts provided opportunities to bring more intense focus on team goals rather than individual goals. In some instances, conflicts helped initiate conversations between and among team members who otherwise may not have interacted in such meaningful ways.

As a case study illustrating factors of conflict competence in a team, we believe the story of the 1980 U.S. Olympic Hockey team provides an excellent example. It's a wonderful bonus that this story has almost mythical proportions. We hope it helps you embrace the potential that is inherent in the conflict your team encounters. And we encourage you to share the story with your teammates, colleagues, and friends.

## So What?

So what now? We've shared the story of the 1980 U.S. Olympic Hockey team. The "Miracle on Ice" has become a symbol for every team striving to achieve its dreams when the odds are stacked against it. The hockey team responded to many challenges, including conflicts, in ways that enabled it to succeed beyond anyone's expectations. We believe every team can learn what it takes to be similarly conflict competent. The necessary ingredients for conflict competence can be identified, examined, and described. That's the good news. But applying and integrating these ingredients, especially when a team is already embroiled in destructive levels of conflict, can be quite difficult. It wasn't easy for the hockey team, and it won't necessarily be easy for your team. The payoffs for taking the challenges however, can be extraordinary. If you are interested in exploring how your team can overcome the destructive impact of conflict, continue reading. If you are intrigued by the notion of tapping into the vast potential inherent in conflict, read on. Even if you're a little skeptical that conflict can be leveraged to your team's advantage, finish reading, and then let your teammates borrow the book. We are excited to share what we've learned about conflict, and we're eager to hear from you once you begin exploring, even embracing, conflict on your team.

We talked with literally hundreds of people in a variety of organizations about conflict in teams. We spoke with executives, officers, general managers, vice presidents, and directors. We also spoke with technicians, players, engineers, service workers, and attendants. We asked them to describe how their teams handled conflicts. We observed their meetings and interactions. We also observed their "meetings after the meeting" and the impact of their intended and unintended communications. We reviewed the research and literature regarding conflict in organizations and between parties. We have spent extensive time in the classroom and in consultation with clients. This book is the culmination of our discussions, observations, research, teaching, and consultations. Our intent is to share what we have learned with you. Let's begin the sharing with a brief overview of what's to come.

## Basic Premise

In our previous book, *Becoming a Conflict Competent Leader*, we suggested that when at least two people are together for any length of time, conflict is inevitable. We offered a behavioral view of conflict based on the work of our colleagues Sal Capobianco, Mark Davis, and Linda Kraus: we suggested that conflict begins with sometimes minor differences and evolves over time. We focused on the fascinating volume of diversity in our organizations. People are different: we have different values, different styles, different personalities, different experiences, and different perspectives. This being the case, we suggested that leaders and anyone aspiring to become a leader be prepared to deal with the inevitable conflicts that arise out of these differences.

We also suggested that conflict can result in positive and negative outcomes. Regarding leaders, we said that conflict exists at the root of some of their best ideas and at the core of many of their worst failures. We believe these same concepts hold true in reference to teams. When handled effectively, conflict within teams can result in surprisingly satisfying outcomes. People are treated with respect. Relationships are strengthened. Conflicts become challenges. Challenges are overcome. Victories are celebrated. Confidence grows. Competence develops.

One significant issue with conflict is that most of us have not learned effective ways to deal with it. In fact, many of us steer clear of conflict at all costs. Others engage passionately in conflict, but in ways that are perceived as hostile, angry, tough, or retaliatory. These two types of behavior, described often as fight-or-flight responses, form the basis for most people's immediate reactions to conflict. Despite these built-in response mechanisms, we can learn to handle conflict more effectively. That's one of the beauties of conflict: effective responses can be learned and applied.

These are our basic premises of conflict:

- Conflict is inevitable.
- Conflict can have both positive and negative results.
- People often use fight-or-flight responses to conflict.
- People can learn more effective conflict skills.

## A Preview: Three Critical Characteristics

This book is intended to help teams and team members assess their current level of conflict competence, select areas for improvement, provide some practical guidance for handling conflicts more effectively, and leverage conflict to their advantage. We focus on practicality over theory. Although we cite some timely scholarly research regarding conflict and present some intriguing data from recent studies, we are committed to examining the consequences of mishandling conflict and the satisfaction in and advantages of constructively managing conflict. This overview of three critical characteristics of conflict competent teams will make our intentions clearer.

### The Right Climate

Trust among teammates is necessary for a team to build conflict competence. Without trust, intentions are misunderstood, aspersions are cast, attributions are made, and assumptions become real. With trust, there is seldom "intention invention" among teammates. Misunderstandings, when they occur, are investigated. Therefore, aspersions and attributions are seldom cast or made. Assumptions are stated clearly, and when they are incorrect, they are quickly resolved.

Trust can be fleeting and fragile if it is not nurtured on a consistent, even deliberate, basis. In Chapter Three we examine the nature of trust in teams. Nearly every person with whom we spoke described trust as the foundation for teams that handle conflict effectively. Specifically, we explore the notion of believing in the good intentions of others as the basis for genuine openness among team members. Vulnerability, far too often described as a weakness, is essential for developing the deepest levels of trust. Of course, in order for team members to show vulnerability, safety is imperative. And what is safe to one team member may not be safe for another. Finally, we look at the role of emotional intelligence as we explore the intricate weaving of trust, vulnerability, and safety in establishing the right climate.

## Behavioral Integration

The essence of complete collaboration has been described by some of our colleagues as "teamness." We're not even sure that *teamness* is a word, especially since our spell-checking software highlights each reference to it in our text and it's not in the dictionary. Nevertheless, we have heard it often enough to use it here. Much of the research on conflict in teams refers to mutuality as a key factor in resolving conflict effectively. Other terms and descriptions that speak to the essence of behavioral integration include *cooperation, collectiveness, joint decision making, togetherness, cohesiveness, shared commitment, shared values,* and *team rewards.* One of our favorite descriptions was that "a conflict competent team comes together and moves together."

In Chapter Three, in addition to discussing the right climate, we explore how teams can achieve teamness or behavioral integration. It is clear to us that establishing the right climate is dependent on behavioral integration, and true behavioral integration is dependent on the right climate. As teams become behaviorally integrated, they discover that they not only handle conflict more effectively, but they are able to take advantage of the opportunities conflict brings to the surface. Differences among team members are valuable building blocks on which new ideas, creative solutions, and unrealized potential can be launched. Teams that become behaviorally integrated are more likely to see their differences and conflicts as advantages and opportunities rather than barriers and traps.

## Constructive Communication

At the root of just about every effective human interaction is communication. Not surprisingly, effective communication is critical to conflict competence in teams. The ways in which teams communicate, the quality of communication, the skill it takes to communicate before, during, and after conflict, and techniques for effective conflict management are discussed in Chapters Four and Five.

Constructive communication, as we describe it, includes what people say and how they say it. In a team environment, communication among team members is akin to the relationship between a person's head and heart. It is the conduit for understanding. The better equipped each member is to communicate constructively, the more likely it is that he or she will address conflict effectively. Therefore, we look at techniques such as devil's advocacy for expanding the opportunities presented by conflict. We examine skills such as empathy and perspective taking for responding to others' emotions and ideas. We suggest ways to use verbal and nonverbal behaviors to cool conflict. Whether repairing destructive conflict or embracing constructive conflict, communication is the vehicle for doing so effectively.

## Another Thing or Two

As we discussed team conflict with other people, we discovered that a variety of special circumstances seemed to crop up in our conversations. For some, these special circumstances were nearly overwhelming. We have devoted Chapter Six to several of these circumstances. Specifically, we consider some of the challenges presented by geographically dispersed teams, culturally diverse teams, and the use of technology in communicating among team members.

Finally, we conclude by offering in Chapter Seven some basic getting-started tips, guidelines, and suggestions. Our hope is that teams will be able to use Chapter Seven for assessing their current level of conflict competence, repairing ongoing conflicts, and strengthening their ability to embrace and take advantage of differences and conflict. The Resources section offers suggestions and recommendations for further exploration and assistance.

# 2

# WHERE CONFLICT COMES FROM, AND WHY IT IS SO HARD TO MANAGE

No one can whistle a symphony; it takes an
orchestra to play it.

—*H. E. Luccock*

Conflict is an integral part of the life of teams. It is inevitable because teams are made up of people and no two people are alike. When people come together, they bring with them different ways of seeing things. When these differences show up, people can feel threatened, and conflict emerges. Interestingly, these same differences can bring excitement and creativity, as well as stress and frustration. In this chapter, we unravel the origin of conflict in teams and explore why it can be so difficult to address.

## Team Models and Conflict

Most major conceptual models of teams recognize the role of conflict, yet they do so in different ways. Katzenbach and Smith (2003) note in *The Wisdom of Teams*, "A team is a small number of people with complementary skills who are committed to a common purpose, performance goals, and approach for which they hold themselves mutually accountable" (p. 45). They create their common purpose through effective communications and constructive conflict. In this case, conflict serves as a catalyst for developing team identity and direction.

From a group developmental perspective Tuckman's stages of forming, storming, norming, and performing represent a model of how teams evolve and present a clear picture of the key role of conflict in this process (Tuckman, 1965). In the storming stage, teams experience intragroup conflict as individuals begin to resist group influence. If successfully resolved, the storming phase leads to a norming stage, where "ingroup feelings and cohesiveness develop, new standards evolve, and new roles are adopted" (p. 396). Ineffectively addressed conflict can impede further team development.

Numerous variations of the group development model have appeared. They usually include a stage where team members experience conflict over goals and procedures. This stage is seen as necessary to develop clarity and trust yet threatening to team unity if the conflict is not well managed (Wheelan, 2005).

Some models view conflict management as a team competency. They recognize that teams inevitably face conflict. Unless it can be resolved effectively, the team will waste considerable time and energy, thus diverting their attention from their main purposes (Dyer, Dyer, Dyer, and Schein, 2007).

In *The Five Dysfunctions of a Team* (2002), Patrick Lencioni presents a model where constructive conflict is an essential component of effective teamwork. When trust is lacking, teams experience the model's second dysfunction: fear of conflict. In this case, team members feel vulnerable and are concerned that others may exploit their weaknesses, so they pull back from rigorous, unfiltered debate of issues. Creativity and sound decision making lag, and team morale and productivity suffer. This leads to the model's third dysfunction, lack of commitment, because team members have not participated in the kind of productive debate that can lead to buy-in and effective implementation of decisions.

Conflict is clearly an important and natural component of team interaction. Before going further, let us look at some of the elements that make conflict such an integral part of the life of teams.

## The Nature of Conflict

In our previous book, we defined conflict as "any situation in which interdependent people have apparently incompatible goals, interests, principles, or feelings" (Runde and Flanagan, 2007, p. 22). Teams are made up of people bound together by common goals. In other words, team members are interdependent; they have to work together to accomplish their objectives. As we will see later in this chapter, any collection of people brings a variety of differences to any situation. Team members have different personalities, preferences, styles, knowledge, experience, interests, needs, perspectives, and values. Sometimes these differences matter very little, if at all. If some prefer to vacation on the beaches of Florida and others prefer the mountains of Colorado, *viva la différence!* At other times, though, differences lead to the appearance of incompatibility, and at this point conflict can emerge. If some team members want to expand operations to a new territory while others think focusing on the existing territory is the better approach, this presents a sense of incompatibility, and conflict starts. This does not mean that the outcome of the conflict will necessarily be bad or good. What happens depends on how the team addresses the differences.

It is easy to see why conflict is inevitable. You have undoubtedly experienced this in your own life and on your own teams. A recent poll by the Center for Creative Leadership found that 85 percent of respondents described the frequency of conflict in their organization as regular or constant, most of which occurred quietly out of sight (McManigle, 2007). Conflict may not be enjoyable, but it is something you will encounter regularly. Our recommendation is to learn how to get the best out of it and at the same time discover how to lessen its harmful effects. For many, this will sound like odd advice. Most will readily agree with reducing conflict's harmful effects; in part, this is why we often try to avoid conflict, thinking that avoidance will lessen the harm (although it usually does not). But getting the best out of conflict is something entirely different. It relates to research on the various ways in which conflict unfolds.

## Types of Conflict

In the 1990s researchers identified two types of organizational conflict. One type focused on personalities and was associated with people trying to find someone to blame for a problem rather than figuring out how to solve it. This conflict has been called by various names: *affective conflict, personality conflict,* and *relationship conflict* (Amason, 1996; Jehn, 1995). We use the term *relationship conflict* to describe this type of conflict that is typified by heightened, negative emotions. It can start quickly and escalate rapidly. It has been widely shown to be associated with poor team productivity and decision making. When we ask people in our programs to share words that come to mind when they think of conflict, they often use negative terms like *frustrating, anger, stressful, fear,* and *wasteful.* These words aptly describe the kinds of feelings and experiences that arise when relationship conflict occurs.

We have all seen this type of conflict. The following story illustrates how easily relationship conflict can flare up and disrupt a team. One team member, Ken, experienced it in a team meeting. Ken and a colleague, Sally, had agreed to wait until the next team meeting to present their different approaches about how the team should allocate resources for a new project. At the beginning of that meeting, Bill, the team leader, led off by presenting a plan for allocating resources that was very similar to Sally's. Almost immediately the following exchange ensued:

> *Ken:* Sally, we agreed to wait until the meeting to discuss our
> different approaches, but it seems you went behind my
> back to talk with Bill.
> *Sally:* What are you talking about! I didn't speak to Bill or any-
> one else about it.

*Ken:* Sure, he just happened to come up with an identical plan.

*Bill:* Hey, Ken; she didn't talk to me about any plan.

*Ken:* You have always favored Sally, and I'm tired of this unfair treatment.

The meeting went downhill from there. The team did not even address the resource allocation question in the meeting. There was plenty of talk afterward, though, most of it dealing with the conflict, not resource allocations. Ken talked to some of his friends on the team to try to get them to take his side. So did Sally. Bill was unsure what to do about the conflict or the resource question. This is an all-too-frequent outcome of relationship conflict. It is easy to see why people associate negative terms like *tension* and *frustration* with this type of conflict.

Researchers called the second type of conflict they identified *cognitive conflict* or *task conflict*. It focuses on the substantive tasks that form the basis for a team's existence. In teams, it is associated with robust debate of issues, heightened creativity that comes from exploring and vetting options, and improved decision making (Roberto, 2005).

In our earlier example, if Bill had opened up the discussion by asking for ideas on how to approach the resource allocation issue, there still might have been conflicting ideas, but they could have been the source for creativity instead of divisiveness. Here's how it might have worked:

*Bill:* I'd like to hear options on how to allocate resources for the project.

*Ken:* I believe we'd be better off keeping the current product mix and using most of our funding on marketing and sales initiatives. The customers I've talked to like the current products. We just need to reach out to them.

*Sally:* That's not the way I see it. The competition is pushing ahead with new product development, and unless we match them, they'll pass us by, and we won't be able to sell our products.

*Ken:* I'm not sure I buy that argument. Can you clarify what competitive threats you're talking about?

*Sally:* Well, I'm particularly concerned with our low-end product line. Reports in the trade press suggest that XYZ Co. is coming out with better-performing models this spring, and they've always been strong competitors on price.

*Ken:* So maybe we could use some of our funds to more aggressively sell our current high-end products and spend some of the rest on upgrading our lower-priced products. If we are successful in selling our high-end products that have good margins, we'll have more money to spend on upgrading all of our products.

There were more disagreements, further exploration of the issues, and new ideas floated. It took time to work things through, but the focus of the conversation was finding solutions to the problem at hand. No one got sidetracked on personal issues.

When our clients describe conflict with terms like *opportunity, challenge, energizing, learning,* and *resolution,* they are basically describing this second kind of conflict, which we call *task conflict* throughout the book. Typically, we get about four times as many words describing relationship conflict as those describing task conflict. This underscores that most people experience conflict as something disagreeable and miss out on the potential opportunities inherent within it. We want to help your team turn this around, so that you get the best out of conflict and at the same time reduce the harmful effects you experience.

Whether conflict is an opportunity or a threat depends on the type of conflict being experienced. And as we will see, this largely depends on the way team members behave when they face conflict. Before that, though, let us explore more about how differences can cause conflict in teams.

## Sources of Conflict

Conflict is inevitable in teams, but what causes it? In this section we explore some of its common sources. This information will help identify ways that teams can manage conflict more effectively.

### Differences

Individuals naturally bring a variety of differences to their teams. These differences can be the sources of creativity, or they can serve to divide. Understanding that they are natural is a first step to dealing with them constructively. Let us look at a variety of differences that often occur among members of teams.

*Personality.* Team members likely have differing personality traits. Some may be open to new ideas and actions, and others may be more comfortable with traditional approaches. Some may be dominant and confident in large groups, while others work quietly in the background. When they are not understood, these and other personality differences can cause discomfort or even lead to suspicion among members.

*Preferences.* People have different preferences for ways of doing things. Some prefer to focus on details, and others like to look at the big picture. The Myers-Briggs Type Indicator is one assessment instrument that helps people understand some of their preferences, as well as become aware of how theirs may differ from those of others. The differences can bring out the best or play to the worst in teams.

*Styles.* If some members on a team approach conflicts with a desire to win, while others seek to avoid them altogether, their stylistic differences themselves can become sources of tension (Thomas and Kilmann, 1974). In problem-solving contexts, some may prefer to maintain current paradigms and work to make things better. Others may be inclined to discard existing models and come up with entirely new solutions. These differences, when not properly understood, can cause conflict when teams try to solve problems (Kirton, 2003).

***Values and Principles.*** Differences in values are at the heart of some of the most difficult conflicts. In some of our programs, we use an exercise that Tim developed called Last Gasp Gorge (Flanagan, 2004). Teams are tasked with developing consensus about the order in which a group of lost hikers will be rescued. The situation is complicated by rising water in a cave that may prevent everyone from being saved. Short biographies are given on each of the lost hikers.

After presenting their personal views of a preferred rescue order, the team members are instructed to reach consensus. Typically a number of different approaches emerge (weakest first, those with the most value to society first, random order, and so forth) that relate to the values of team members. Although this is just an exercise, the discussions can get quite heated, particularly when a participant's values are challenged. In real life, team members' value differences can also lead to sharp conflict.

***Cultural Differences.*** Cultural differences can lead to conflict, as well as complicate its resolution. People from various cultures often have different views about how things should be done. Some cultures value individualism, while others prefer a collectivist approach. Members from individualist cultures may prefer a system that favors rewarding high-performing members of the team. Members from collectivist cultures may prefer team-based rewards. These differences can easily cause members to become irritated with others.

Different cultures also have varying approaches to resolving conflict. Some prefer to deal directly with the issue. This is typically the approach in North America and northern Europe.

Other cultures, including many in Asia, prefer to be less direct, even delivering messages through third parties. Some cultures prefer to be expressive about emotions associated with conflict, while others are more restrained (Hammer, 2003). In our multicultural world, these differences can create problems.

At a recent conference in China, I (Craig) participated in discussions about conflict with businesspeople from around the world. One common story concerned North American managers talking with their Asian counterparts about a conflict. The North Americans were confused when their Asian colleagues appeared to agree with a particular point, only to act differently later. From the Asian managers' viewpoint, they were not agreeing but rather being courteous by not directly challenging their colleagues. Unless team members are aware of these kinds of culturally related differences, they can exacerbate conflict even as people try to resolve it.

**Knowledge and Experience.** Differences in members' knowledge or experience can bring strength and flexibility to a team. They can also lead to conflict when these differences lead one person to advocate strategies or tactics that another person does not understand. In these situations, it is important to try to learn what is behind the other person's perspective in order to benefit from his or her knowledge and experience.

**Interests and Needs.** Team members usually have different interests and needs. On project teams, some team members may have divided interests between what is good for the team and what is good for their home department. In other settings, there are team members who may see the team as a stepping-stone for their own careers or feel the need for special recognition, while others are more interested in team success. Two fellow team members may both be interested in fulfilling the same role. So a variety of interests or needs may show up as differences in the team and serve as a source for conflict.

*Goals.* Clarifying goals is crucial for team success. When members have different ideas about what a team's goals should be, conflict can arise. Effective communications can lead to a deeper shared understanding and commitment to goals. But when discussion is avoided and goals remain ambiguous, successful team functioning can be undermined.

## Feelings of Incompatibility

Regardless of the kinds of differences that appear, conflict arises only if the people involved sense that their differences are somehow incompatible. Sometimes the mere appearance of incompatibility is all that is needed. Even when we are mistaken or misinterpret what another person has said, it can be enough to spark conflict. Consider the following example.

Mary was irritated that Allen wanted to spend most of the advertising budget on print media, when most of their new customers were coming from the Internet. She had heard that he had been soliciting bids from print advertisers, even though the best answer was to boost their electronic marketing efforts. It was just like Allen to get stuck in old patterns. When Mary finally talked to Allen about the issue, she expressed her irritation. If they had not been able to calm down and talk things out, she might never have learned that Allen actually agreed with her. He had solicited the print bids to bolster arguments to senior management that electronic marketing would provide a better return on investment for their product line than comparable investments in print ads.

## Unmet Expectations

When people have expectations about how others will think and act, they are often surprised and frustrated when these expectations are not met. These expectation violations can create negative emotions that can trigger destructive reactions. This can happen even if our expectations are unclear or unrealistic or we have not shared our expectations with the other person (Dyer, Dyer, Dyer, and Schein, 2007).

Barry liked to get projects done ahead of schedule in order to have a buffer if something went wrong. Chris, who worked for Barry, worked better under pressure and preferred to wait until closer to the deadline to gear up. Barry grew frustrated with Chris even though they had never talked about how Barry liked regular progress reports and early completion targets.

## Complicating Factors

Team conflict can arise when we sense incompatibility or our expectations are not met. It takes place between team members, a team leader and a team member, subgroups within a team, or different teams. It can be task focused or relationship focused. In other words, team conflict is complex.

Time and resource pressures can exacerbate conflict. When deadlines are short, people typically revert to their preferred behavior patterns and are less likely to listen well to others. This can cause natural differences to turn into difficult conflicts. When resources are limited, people's efforts to get what they need can clash with others' needs.

One of our clients, a regional vice president of sales for a consumer goods distributor, strongly believed that listening to others' concerns was critically important in times of conflict. Nevertheless, he found it difficult to actually do this. When conflicts emerged and decisions needed to be made quickly, he would often jump into decision-making mode and forget to listen to others. He found, though, that when he acted this way, problems resurfaced later. Although he dealt with them quickly, he was not always getting to the root of problems. It took effort, but over time he was able to change his approach. He consciously made himself slow down and ask questions of his managers. He stopped falling back on habitual patterns even when the pressure was on.

He began to listen more carefully and make decisions that addressed both the short- and long-term aspects of problems.

In addition to these factors, conflict involves emotion. When people feel that their interests are threatened, they often become emotional and respond ineffectively to the conflict. They may tend to pull back in the face of conflict. Do you talk more or less to someone with whom you are experiencing conflict? If you are like most other people, you will talk less with him or her. If so, are you more or less likely to resolve conflict? Probably less. This and many other elements complicate conflict and make it a challenge for individuals and teams.

## Challenges

When we ask people who attend our programs why they have such a hard time dealing with conflict, their most common response is that they never learned how. Very few people learn how to respond to conflict in school or at work. New programs in mediation and conflict resolution in middle and high schools are encouraging, but it will be a while before their results are felt in the workplace. Most people get their training by watching others who never received any training either.

On top of this, conflict is often full of emotions that make it difficult to sort through the issues in a rational manner. Even in individual conflicts, things can get messy and confusing in a hurry. When the complexity of team interactions is added to the mix, it is easy to see why team conflict can be such a challenge. It is also understandable that many teams do not make the best out of the conflicts and all too often get the worst. Such results are not inevitable, though. In this section, we look at team conflict more closely to help you understand what makes it so complex and difficult to manage. Understanding the challenge will lead to discoveries about what teams need to do to be able to deal with conflict more effectively.

## Task Conflict

Researchers have long recognized that there are different types of conflict. One type, task conflict, concerns disagreements among team members about the work they are performing. It evolves from the natural differences of ideas and opinions that occur among people. This type of conflict, when managed well, can improve the performance of teams (Jehn, 1995).

The makeup of teams can contribute to the occurrence of task conflict. Typically when teams consist of people with a wide variety of opinions about issues that confront the team, the likelihood of task conflict increases. This can occur when team members have different educational backgrounds, areas of functional specialty, and values. It often occurs in larger teams because the greater number of team members encompasses more diversity (Mooney, Holahan, and Amason, 2007).

Researchers have found that task conflict can often help teams be more creative and make better decisions. They are able to be more creative because task conflict exposes people to differing ideas, causes them to reflect on other approaches and promotes learning that can be particularly effective with non-routine issues (Chen, 2006). Teams can make better decisions because they question assumptions, debate the merits of different approaches, and develop a synthesis that is better than any one member's ideas. When teams do not have enough task conflict, they usually render poorer-quality decisions (Amason, 1996; Roberto, 2005).

Although task conflict can have positive outcomes for a team, it is important to know when and how to use it. It tends to be easier to work with task conflict when dealing with situations that are less provocative and less likely to lead to emotional tensions (Edmondson and Smith, 2006).

Even in the right circumstance, the team leader needs to make sure that task conflict unfolds at the right level of intensity. When there is not enough task conflict or if it takes place at too low a level of intensity, the team typically experiences lackluster decision making and performance. The team will not have enough discussion, debate, and vetting of ideas. At the other end of the spectrum, task conflict that becomes too intense can begin to change into relationship conflict, with its associated negative outcomes. When debate gets too heated, it becomes easy for people to start taking comments personally and for emotions to get triggered. At that point, people begin having difficulty focusing on the issue at hand. Researchers have found that moderate levels of intensity in task conflict result in better outcomes (De Dreu, 2006).

## Relationship Conflict

Relationship conflict centers more on who is to blame than on how to solve the problem. It arises when team members become angry with one another and begin to see each other as the problem. Mistrust and dissension arise, causing team cohesion to weaken. It is critical, but never easy, to deal with relationship conflict.

When team members have different values, relationship conflict can easily emerge (Jehn, Chadwick, and Thatcher, 1997). It often arises when the issues at hand address important concerns or hot topics. When a team reaches an impasse, the situation can get personal, and relationship conflict can emerge (Edmondson and Smith, 2006).

People often try to avoid dealing with relationship conflict because it is so troublesome. In some cases, it may be beneficial to hold off dealing with it in the short term in order to enable team members to complete their work. In most cases though, particularly over the long term, avoidance is harmful. Since it is impossible to completely avoid relationship conflict, the ability to deal with it effectively when it does emerge is essential.

## Process Conflict

Researchers have identified one other type of conflict: process conflict (Jehn, 1995). It deals with team member differences about how they should work together to accomplish certain tasks. Teams must address it, especially in the early phases of the team's life. If team members cannot make decisions about how they want to go about their business, this impasse can cripple their ability to move ahead effectively. We will not spend much time on this type of conflict because it is not as well researched. We do suggest, however, that teams can address process conflict in similar ways to the manner they handle task and relationship conflict.

## How Task Conflict Morphs into Relationship Conflict

In many ways, it seems as if the best recommendation for teams should be to just engage in appropriate levels of task conflict and stay away from relationship conflict. It is just not that easy. When teams begin to engage in task conflict, the situation often gets out of hand. What was once a debate about the best ways to approach a particular issue suddenly becomes personalized attacks on one another. Task conflict is often the starting point of relationship conflict, so the better question for teams is, "How can we use task conflict while at the same time lessening the chances that it will change into relationship conflict?"

This is quite a challenge because when task conflict begins to get intense or addresses hot topics, it easily transforms into relationship conflict. People begin looking at criticisms of their ideas as criticisms of themselves, and then they get angry (De Dreu, 2006).

## Attribution

One of the reasons that task conflict turns into relationship conflict concerns a concept called *attribution*. Attribution refers to the way one person interprets or assumes the motives behind someone else's actions. When we see someone do or say something, particularly something we do not like, we think about what caused the person to behave that way. We often attribute bad motives to the other person, even though that was not his or her intention. For example, if someone criticizes our comments or thoughts in a debate, we may think she is trying to get her own way by disparaging us.

The process of attribution is fraught with potential errors. Often people attribute worse motives to others than they actually have. In particular, we may attribute someone's actions to character, as opposed to circumstances that may have been beyond his control. Attributions that place blame on someone based on character are called *dispositional attributions*. Attributions related to circumstances beyond another person's control are called *situational attributions*. In general, people tend to attribute other people's actions to dispositional causes. This leads to negative feelings toward the other person. We become angry at him for doing what he did, because we think it was his intention to hurt us or to take advantage of us (Allred, 2000).

Other elements affect attributions too. Sometimes we attribute sinister motives to others based on stereotypes. If a person is a member of a particular group, we may automatically assume a particular intent even without considering the person's unique viewpoints or circumstances.

When we are in a bad mood or our emotions have been aroused for other reasons, we more readily attribute dubious motives to another person (Jordan and Troth, 2004). People also have certain things that tend to set them off. When a person acts in one of these ways that push our hot buttons, it can stimulate negative attributions that stir emotions and may lead to relationship conflict. This is particularly true when we are dealing with people with whom we have had a history of conflict. In these situations, when the other person acts in a certain way, we are much more likely to attribute bad motives to him or her and get angry as a result. Finally, bad behaviors on the part of other people, such as use of harsh language, personal attacks, and intimidation, can lead to negative attributions and the emotions that stem from them (Simons and Peterson, 2000).

These behaviors are threatening to most people and quickly evoke fight-or-flight responses that contribute to relationship conflict.

## Social Judgment

Social judgment is another factor that can cause task conflict to turn into relationship conflict. This has to do with the way in which leaders sometimes make decisions. Because they are very busy, decision makers often lack the time to fully explain the basis for their decisions. Others can easily read into the decisions motives that are different from what the leader actually intended. If they do not like a particular judgment, they may attribute the decision to something other than a rational process; for example, they may think that it was made for political reasons. These kinds of assessments can make people angry and steer what otherwise may be task conflict into relationship conflict (Mooney, 2007).

When people attribute bad motives to someone else's decision or action, they usually feel anger and other negative emotions. In effect, they feel that they have been attacked or their wishes have been thwarted. They blame the other person for purposely doing this and feel that the other person should pay (Allred, 2000).

## Behavioral Responses

When people get angry during conflict, especially relationship conflict, they typically resort to one of two types of responses: fight or flight. Long ago these behaviors helped humans keep safe when they faced a threat. Our biological and neurological systems evolved to enable us to deal with such crises. In modern life, however, these fight-or-flight responses are usually ineffective in dealing with conflict with teammates. Our teammates are people with whom we have ongoing, interdependent relationships, and fight-or-flight responses do not support those relationships. The fight behaviors involve beating, putting down, or getting back at the other person. Some flight behaviors are staying away from the other person, giving in, and doing whatever is necessary to avoid addressing the conflict. In both cases, fight and flight, these destructive behaviors generate unproductive outcomes.

Another behavioral approach people use is venting their frustrations to others. Sometimes letting off steam can be helpful to relieve some of the pressure and tension associated with conflict. In general, however, this type of response does not lessen the conflict. Sometimes it actually increases people's anger as they ruminate on the bad things the other person did. They will often get support from others that they feel justifies their anger and causes them to behave in ways that result in escalating conflict (Allred, 2000).

Responding to your emotional reactions with fight-or-flight behaviors can set in motion escalatory or retaliatory cycles. One person responds to another's behavior, which begets a response in kind, and the retaliatory cycle begins. Sometimes it is called a *retaliatory spiral*, because each response becomes more intense. The second response is more heated than the first, and the third more heated still. This cycle exacerbates relationship conflict in teams (Dana, 2005; Wilmot and Hocker, 2001).

In reality, both task and relationship conflict are almost always present in some varying proportions. When task conflict represents a higher proportion of the overall conflict than relationship conflict, people are usually less tense and team outcomes are generally better. When relationship conflict represents the greater proportion of conflict, then emotions run high, and teams have greater difficulty in resolving the conflict. So it is not a matter of totally doing away with one or the other, but managing the amount of conflict so that overall, there is more constructive task conflict than destructive relationship conflict (Jehn and Chatman, 2000).

Teams need to learn how to get the benefits out of task conflict without experiencing the harm of relationship conflict. To do so, they must learn how to develop new operating norms and approaches that will provide a better basis for handling conflict.

## Conflict Norms

We talked with many team members, coaches, and consultants in researching this book. One theme that resonated through all their comments is that teams struggle with conflict when they do not pay attention to how they want to address it. Most teams focus on the tasks for which they are formed. This is natural. Unfortunately, they spend relatively little time on how they want to work together. They do not address how they want to handle conflict when it arises, and make no mistake, it will arise. Too many teams do not take the time to create the norms of conduct that will help them manage conflict effectively.

Fortunately, researchers have carefully studied the kinds of norms that teams can adopt to improve their handling of conflict. These have included developing new attitudes toward conflict, fostering openness and cohesiveness, and improving emotional intelligence. Teams that develop effective norms and approaches for handling conflict can create the right environment for addressing conflicts constructively.

*New Attitudes.* The most successful teams are ones that develop a focus on being productive (Katzenbach and Smith, 2003). This includes recognizing that conflict is going to be an inevitable part of team life and that it can be used to contribute to the team's productivity (Chen, 2006). It does this because when task conflict is properly managed, new ideas can be uncovered, alternatives can be explored and vetted, and the team can build a stronger cohesiveness and commitment that will help in implementing new ideas. Effective use of task conflict can also promote creativity and innovation because new ideas are brought to the surface, and the interactions of people with different viewpoints can stimulate new thoughts that may be better than any of the original ones (Amason, Thompson, Hochwarter, and Harrison, 1995).

Teams also need to recognize that engaging conflict is more effective than avoiding it. Most teams we meet tend to avoid conflict—sometimes at all costs. We recommend they work on changing their attitude toward conflict so they no longer avoid it but instead engage it constructively using solutions-oriented approaches. One way to do this is to use an approach that separates the people from the problem, with the debates focused on issues, not participants (Fisher, Ury, and Patton, 1991). Another approach is to search for win-win solutions where everyone benefits. Finally, teams should incorporate a process to make sure that when people are hurt by conflict, the team quickly addresses the matter to achieve reconciliation and make the team whole again. As conflict management expert William Ury notes in *The Third Side* (2000), conflict is not fully resolved until damaged relationships have begun to heal.

*Openness.* To be effective in addressing conflict, teams need to be tolerant of different viewpoints and encourage direct expressions of differences (Amason and Sapienza, 1997; Lovelace, Shapiro, and Weingart, 2001). This involves accepting that there will be differences and acknowledging that these can be valuable to the team. With this recognition, team members can then work to keep an open mind so that they can be persuaded when new or better ideas emerge (Schultz-Hardt, Jochims, and Frey, 2002).

Openness obviously depends on building trust among team members, and trust means being willing to take risks with one another and to be vulnerable. It is based on a sense that the other members of the team have the best interests of each other in mind (Mooney, Holahan, and Amason, 2007). Openness also depends on the development of psychological safety, meaning that team members feel safe to participate in debates knowing that their colleagues will not use what they say against them (Edmondson and Smith, 2006).

*Cohesiveness.* Another area for norm development concerns cohesiveness—how well the team sticks together to work through conflict. This means that team members have a sense of mutuality, the feeling that they are jointly responsible and accountable for the goals and consequences of the team (Amason and Sapienza, 1997). It also includes the way that teams engage in mutual and collective interaction (Mooney, 2007; Hambrick, 1998). It encompasses sharing information and resources, obtaining clarity on goals and roles, making decisions together, and developing team rewards as opposed to individual ones. It also looks at the ways and frequencies with which team members cooperate with one another (Yeatts and Hyten, 1998; Eisenhardt, Kehwajy, and Bourgeois, 1997a).

*Emotional Intelligence.* Improved emotional intelligence can help team members be more effective in dealing with their own emotions around conflict as well as those of their colleagues. It involves the ability of team members to be aware of their emotions, acknowledge them, and manage them effectively (Edmondson and Smith, 2006). It also encompasses the ability to cool down, slow down, and reflect on what is happening. Emotionally intelligent team members are aware of their colleagues' emotions and perceptions related to conflicts, and this enables them to respond more effectively to them.

## Addressing the Challenges

In the rest of the book, we are going to look at how team leaders and team members can address the challenges presented by the complexities of conflict. This is about developing the right team climate to enable open communications and then using constructive communication techniques when debating and discussing issues. Figure 2.1 illustrates the elements that go into each of the components of building conflict competent teams.

In Chapter Three, we examine how teams can create the right climate for managing conflict effectively. This involves developing more effective attitudes about conflict, deepening trust, developing psychological safety, working collaboratively and cohesively as a team (behavioral integration), and improving emotional intelligence.

In Chapters Four and Five, we explore how teams can use constructive communication behaviors (reflective thinking and delay responding, listening for understanding, perspective taking, and expressing emotions) and techniques to address conflict. We also review how to avoid falling into the destructive fight-or-flight behaviors so common in teams. While teams need

## Figure 2.1 Components for Building Conflict Competent Teams

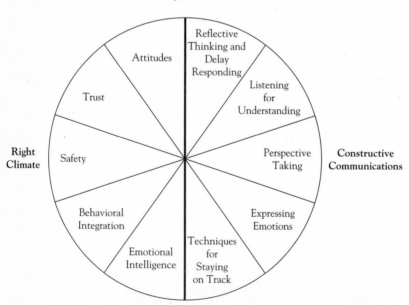

the right climate, they also need team members to be able to listen effectively to one another and communicate in constructive, noncontentious manners (DeChurch and Marks, 2001).

In each of these chapters, we also look at the roles team leaders can play to help their teams become more effective: modeling constructive behaviors, being aware of and managing their emotions and those of their team members, repairing hurt feelings when necessary, and facilitating openness and trust. In these ways, team leaders can influence the course of conflict so that it can provide productive outcomes for their teams.

# Components for Building Conflict Competent Teams

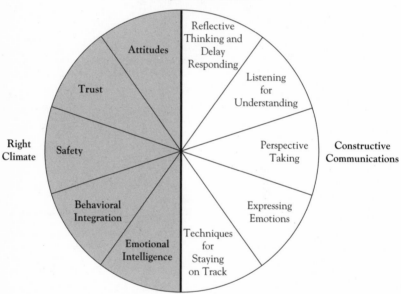

# 3

# CREATING THE RIGHT CLIMATE

Finding good players is easy. Getting them to play
as a team is another story.

—*Casey Stengel*

We have seen that conflict is inevitable, complex, and emotionally challenging for teams. In order to deal effectively with conflict, teams need to be able to create a climate where team members feel safe to be open with one another. They need to be able to approach conflict with a positive attitude. They have to be able to trust one another and work together closely. Finally, they need to be aware of and sensitive to emotional issues that arise during conflict. Before examining these elements more closely, it will be helpful to examine a situation where a team operated in the wrong climate.

Our story comes from a support department at a Fortune 100 company. The division's long-term director preferred to lead by intimidation. Members of his top management team did what they were told, which contributed to an environment of dependency. The managers were kept in the dark about why decisions were being made. Trust was low, and no one ever knew what to expect next. The managers felt it was better to keep quiet and not share information lest it be used against them.

Employees in the department began to take an adversarial approach toward management, in part because they did not receive answers about why actions were being taken that created perceived inequities over scheduling and other policies. When conflicts initially arose, employees discussed them with their managers. After numerous frustrating interactions, they began taking their complaints directly to the human resources (HR) department. When HR confronted the director and managers with these complaints, more comprehensive reasons were provided for their decisions. Unfortunately, these were not shared with the employees earlier in the process.

A new manager, Fran, was placed in the department. She was given the task of improving production in one key area of the department. It was immediately evident that her new department was laboring under a negative conflict climate. People were not talking to one another, but they did talk a great deal behind their colleagues' backs. In meetings, there was little debate about issues, and people seemed guarded.

Little did Fran know that she would soon replace the old director and assume the responsibility of turning things around. One of her first challenges was changing the climate by addressing attitudes, trust, safety, collaboration, and the emotional intelligence of the management team.

## Effective Attitudes

As we have seen, people often look at conflict negatively. They have probably experienced conflict as troubling or distressing in their personal and professional lives. In large measure, this is because they have never learned the skills needed to deal with conflict effectively, so it remains troublesome.

One of the first things that a team can do to begin creating the right climate is for team members to share assumptions and attitudes that they have toward conflict. This conversation can be intimidating because conflict often brings up emotional issues. By looking at why we feel the way we do about conflict, some of the mystery can be taken out of conflict, and it becomes more approachable. It is helpful not only to look at some of the more distressing elements of conflict that people experience, but also to consider the experiences in our lives when conflict has actually been productive. By focusing on some of the aspects of conflict that can be helpful to the team, it becomes possible to begin changing attitudes so that conflict is not always seen as something negative.

We recommend beginning by looking at conflict as holding the potential for helping people come up with better ideas. If we are able to deal with it effectively, conflict and the differences underlying it can serve as a basis for creative explorations of issues and developing better decisions and higher levels of commitment for implementing them. If attitudes toward conflict go unspoken and fears or concerns remain hidden, then when conflict arises, people are more likely to avoid it and lose out on these opportunities. They are also more likely to engage it in ineffective ways because they are scared of it. When this happens, it brings out the worst elements of conflict and causes the team to suffer.

When Fran came into her new department, the prevailing attitude of the management team toward conflict was to avoid it at all costs. As a consequence, issues were not debated. The director made decisions, but he did not benefit from the discussion and vetting of ideas that comes from task conflict. Relationships between employees and managers were strained because problems were not openly addressed.

Shortly after she arrived, issues came to a head. The old director was forced out, and Fran was named to replace him. She had a different attitude toward conflict and saw the opportunities that it could bring. She began talking with each member of the management team to get their take on how to deal with the conflicts in the department. As a result of these discussions, she learned a lot about how the individuals she worked with viewed conflict. This also helped her recognize which managers were upset that she had been named the director. She continued talking with her team to see whether they would be able to adjust to the new setting. All but two of the eight stayed.

In subsequent team meetings, Fran began discussing how she wanted the managers to be more open in talking about conflicts.

She shared ways in which conflict could help the team come up with better options and make superior decisions. She asked managers to share stories about when conflicts had resulted in better outcomes for them personally. They were reluctant at first but finally came up with some examples and began to see that things would be changing. Conflict had always been around and probably always would be, but perhaps they could make something positive out of it. First, they needed to learn to trust one another.

## Trust

A recent *Fortune* magazine article noted, "Trust is the most fundamental element of a winning team" (Colvin, 2006, p. 87). Developing a trusting environment can make all the difference in helping teams bring out the best and avoid the worst elements of conflict. We will look at what trust is and how it makes a difference in creating the right climate for effective conflict management in teams.

Trust is so important in creating the right climate because it enables members of a team to risk being open and honest with one another. It enables people to challenge each other, debate issues, and say what they think needs to be said. When trust is high, people believe that they can depend on one another to respond in ways that safeguard each other's interests.

### The Nature of Trust and Trustworthiness

Most commentators agree that trust is a person's willingness to be vulnerable with another even though he or she cannot control the other person's responses (Mayer and Gavin, 2005). Others suggest that there are different types of trust. One type is trust in one's self: a sense of being competent to carry out tasks and the integrity and willingness to do the right thing.

Another is trust in other people. This kind of one-on-one trust means believing that another person has your interests at heart and is able to act on that intent. A third is trust in an organization or a team. High trust on a team encourages shared information and creates a positive culture where people are honest with each other (Covey and Merrill, 2006).

In order for people to trust others, they have to feel that the other person is trustworthy. Research has suggested that trustworthiness has three elements: ability, benevolence, and integrity. Ability alludes to other persons having the skill and competence to be able to deliver and complete what they have said they will. Benevolence is the belief that the other person cares about you. Integrity means the other person adheres to principles that you find acceptable (Mayer and Gavin, 2005). When you feel someone else is trustworthy, you become willing to take risks and be honest with that person. You can show vulnerability because you feel confident that she or he will not take advantage of you. Another element of trustworthiness is loyalty—a sense that a person has your best interests in mind and will stay faithful to them. A felt sense of loyalty enables people to be willing to dissent, speak up, and disagree in team settings. This is crucial because it enables differences to be aired and ideas vetted. When ideas can be bounced off team members, differences become the basis for creative action (Dooley and Fryxell, 1999).

**Ability to Trust.** Our capacity to trust influences our willingness to take risks, be open with other people, and appreciate differences. Trust is affected by a number of elements, including people's attitudes, values, and even their moods. People who share similar values more easily feel trust toward one another. When values differ, they must make additional efforts to reach out and learn enough about the other person to enable trust to grow.

Sometimes our attitudes toward others affect our ability to trust. We may let stereotypes influence our views. We may also be affected by how we have seen the other person in different contexts or even what we have heard others say about them. These types of attitudes are clearly evaluative in nature, as are the attributions we sometimes make.

Even our moods and emotions can affect our ability or willingness to trust. Feeling strong emotions tends to interrupt people's ability to think clearly, and often it affects their ability to be able to trust others—at least as long as the emotions remain high. Emotions color our experience and affect whether we can suspend our beliefs long enough to experience how the other person actually behaves. When we are in a bad mood, we have more difficulty giving the other person the benefit of the doubt and avoid making attributions based on those emotions.

Trust in team leaders is particularly important in team settings. Trusting the leader allows members to suspend their personal doubts, and work more easily toward a common goal (Allred, 2000). Team members can focus on tasks and have a positive influence on team performance. When leaders are seen as trustworthy, team members can be more attentive to each other and more openly express opinions (Elsbach, 2004). Behaviors that managers can use to strengthen trust among team members include being consistent in their behaviors, telling the truth, showing that they care about others, and communicating with a sense of integrity.

**The Importance of Trust in Conflict.** As Patrick Lencioni suggests in *The Five Dysfunctions of a Team* (2002), trust enables team members to be willing to show vulnerability and overcome their fear of conflict. When you feel that other team members care about you and have your best interests at heart, you know that if you take a risk or show weakness, they will not penalize you. There is risk involved in a number of the key constructive behaviors associated with conflict. Behaviors such as perspective taking, expressing emotions, and reaching out pose risks: risks of finding out information you do not want to know, risks of looking weak, and risks of being rebuffed for trying to get discussions moving again. Research with clients at the Leadership Development Institute at Eckerd College has demonstrated that these types of risks are exactly the kind that conflict competent leaders are willing to take (Capobianco, Davis, and Kraus, 2005). Research has also demonstrated that trust contributes to more robust communication sharing, which is critical when dealing with conflict (Chowdhery, 2005).

## Building Trust

A number of elements go into building trust. Stephen Covey Jr. suggests that a motive of caring will do more than anything else to build credibility and trust (Covey and Merrill, 2006). Integrity, honesty, and courage all play a part. Yet people believing that you have their best interests at heart—or at least that you will not harm them when they show vulnerability—is the key. When conflict occurs, this means being willing to tell the other person how you feel. It also requires respecting and listening carefully to how he or she feels and not talking about others behind their backs. In conflict, it is easy to avoid speaking to someone with whom you disagree or are angry. Instead we speak to others on the team about that individual. Of course, this conversation gets back to the person, and when it does, trust has been lost. It is also lost when people's vulnerability is used against them. If someone admits a weakness or expresses vulnerability in some manner, perhaps by expressing emotions about how he or she feels, it is essential not to take advantage of that person. Building trust between individuals involves talking straight with them, telling them how you feel, and being willing to admit that you are wrong. You have to be willing to listen to their side of the story and show respect for them. You also need to give them the benefit of the doubt, while at the same time holding both them and yourself accountable for agreements that you make.

Trust takes courage—the courage to be personally responsible for your actions and willing to take the risk of listening to others and sharing your own ideas and feelings rather than hiding them. This courage will enable you to engage in the kinds of debates that raise necessary issues, clarify expectations, and explore new ground.

Trust comes from experience. Trust grows when people have shared experiences with other team members and have seen how others follow through on their promises. It grows when colleagues show concern for the welfare of each other.

A major role of a leader is to foster situations where people have the opportunity to get to know one another better and begin to develop trust. The team leader can show the way by demonstrating vulnerability. She can do this by reaching out when communications are stuck and sharing emotions associated with conflict. There are obviously associated risks, but they are ones a leader will take to ensure that conflict is managed effectively. By taking these risks, the leader encourages team members to do the same.

When Fran took over, her management team had very low trust. The former director had manipulated people so frequently that everyone was afraid to share anything with others for fear of losing their own position. They were in a low-communication, low-trust environment. The same situation held true for relationships between employees and the managers. Fran knew this had to change if they were going to be able to deal with conflict more effectively.

Her individual talks with the members of the management team were a good start. She learned more about how people had communicated in the past. She told the managers that she wanted to find a way to improve the level of trust in the team. After that, Fran hired a consultant to help work on team building. The consultant used a series of exercises to give the managers a chance to get to know one another better and work together on challenges in a safe environment. It provided them with a fun, nonintimidating way of learning that they could count on their colleagues.

Trust was not a quick fix, though. It took time for the members of the team to learn that they could take risks and not have others take advantage of them. Fran made sure she was the first one to take risks. She tried things that might fail and expressed her feelings about situations, even though there was a risk of looking weak.

She also started meeting with employees. They were understandably skeptical given their experience with management. She told them that she wanted to change the way things worked and wanted their direct involvement. She included them in efforts to develop new policies that were even-handed and backed up her words with action. When employees came up with an innovative approach to solving scheduling issues, Fran supported it and made sure it was implemented. This early victory helped begin to change employees' attitudes and improve their sense of trust.

## Repairing Trust When It Has Been Betrayed

Trust is so important that leaders and team members must make sure that when there has been a breach, they address it right away. When someone has taken advantage of another or has not demonstrated concern for others' well-being, the issue cannot be allowed to fester. When trust is breached, people begin to make negative attributions toward others. This leads to more relationship conflict and diminishes the team's ability to use task conflict effectively.

People assess breaches of trust from both a cognitive and an affective standpoint. They look at what happened and think about why people took the actions they did. They also respond emotionally, often with anger. When attributions become negative, emotions follow suit. The more negative they become, the more likely trust will erode. Sometimes a single breach will be forgiven, but multiple breaches are almost never overlooked

(Elangovan, Werner, and Szabo, 2007). Leaders need to make sure that when breaches happen, they are addressed quickly.

When addressing breaches, we need to be able to observe and acknowledge what has happened, then allow feelings to surface and be examined. The person who breached trust must take responsibility and apologize. The person whose trust has been breached needs to determine whether to forgive the other person and move on. In every case, speed is of the essence (Roberto, 2005).

Fran's team was not immune to breaches of trust. In the beginning, it happened all too often. She knew these could undermine all that she was working toward, so she acted fast to address them. If she made a mistake that could jeopardize trust, she was quick to apologize and make amends. If one of the managers talked to her about another manager, she quickly got them together to work out any disagreements face-to-face. In the early days, she encountered more of these situations because people had been unaccustomed to building or maintaining trust. As time went on and the managers began to feel that their colleagues "had their backs," there were fewer breaches, and trust grew.

## Safety

Trust enables people to be vulnerable. It helps them manage risk and be more open and willing to talk with others. As a consequence, it helps teams use task conflict more effectively. It also lessens the likelihood that task conflict will change into relationship conflict. Trust is usually something that develops between two people. A similar concept, *psychological safety*, focuses on groups. Like trust, it allows people in groups to be able to share ideas and collaborate with others readily. Psychological safety involves trust, as well as mutual respect.

Developed by Amy Edmondson from Harvard Business School, the concept of psychological safety focuses on how individuals feel. It is concerned with short-term consequences and deals with whether team members feel safe taking risks within the team. It is similar to trust, but whereas trust is more focused on relationships between two people, safety deals more with the sense of trust or willingness to take a risk with an entire group (Edmondson, 2004). Psychological safety is a belief that team members will not embarrass, reject, or punish you for speaking up. It enables people to open up and learn more, because it lessens their concerns about the potential reactions of others.

Leaders also have an important role in developing safety within a team. Since trust and mutual respect are keys in building psychological safety, leaders need to make sure that both are present. They have to demonstrate openness themselves, and they need to coach others in order to create a safe atmosphere. Leaders have to make sure that when someone does show vulnerability in the team, no one else takes advantage of it. Leaders need to be approachable, invite input, and promote the willingness of team members to take risks and even to fail (Edmondson, 2004). When psychological safety is established, team members become more willing to speak up about their concerns, seek help, and push boundaries. They become more willing to debate issues, express their dissent, and encourage others to do the same.

At the same time that Fran worked to promote trust between individuals on her management team, she tried to create an environment where the managers could feel safe talking candidly about issues with the team. The team expressly addressed the importance of being frank with one another and looked at obstacles that would prevent them from doing so. They came up with specific norms that addressed safety. First, they agreed to be candid and tell each other how they really thought or felt about issues. Second, they affirmed that any member of the team who disagreed with another would speak directly with that person, and not behind his or her back. Finally, they agreed that no one would take advantage of someone else's comments or use them against the person. The rules applied to all of them, and they agreed to hold each other accountable for them.

## Working Together

In addition to developing trust and psychological safety, teams that seek to deal effectively with conflict need to work together closely. A collaborative spirit enables team members to better understand one another and open up to each other. The formal term researchers use for this collaborative atmosphere is *behavioral integration*. It encompasses sharing information in a rich, accurate, and timely manner; working together; and making decisions together. In essence, it means acting like a team (Hambrick, 1998). When team members work together closely and have a high level of behavioral integration, the links between task and relationship conflict begin to weaken. When team members know how to work together, they begin to give each other the benefit of the doubt. When they do so, they are less likely to attribute bad motives to each other, and task conflict is less likely to morph into relationship conflict.

Behavioral integration is particularly helpful when teams deal with new challenges and need to engage in task conflict to come up with novel resolutions of problems. In these settings, working together closely helps them explore and debate issues without matters becoming personal (Carmeli and Schaubroeck, 2006). When a leader has a strong sense of the importance of collective interaction, it becomes easier for the team to work closely (Simsek, Lubatkin, Veiga, and Dino, 2005). Trust and safety can help enable closer working relationships in teams because people feel more comfortable; they know that their colleagues will not likely let them down or take advantage when they take a risk. With all this in mind, team leaders should stress the need for openness. They can encourage the team to adopt a norm for open communication and information sharing. Leaders need to stay away from holding covert meetings and keeping people out of the loop. They have to resist the temptation to have all communications and decisions run through them.

Team-building exercises can help strengthen collaborative skills and sentiments. Emphasizing joint norm setting, problem solving, and decision making can reinforce them (Hambrick, 1998). From a structural viewpoint, keeping teams small enables people to work together regularly. Allowing periodic turn-over in team membership can bring fresh perspectives to bear. Allocating at least some of the rewards and recognition based on team performance keeps the focus on joint objectives.

When Fran joined the department, the management team was for all purposes behaviorally disintegrated. All significant communications ran through the director, and he made all deci-sions. Team members did not collaborate, share information, or even support one another.

Fran vowed to change this. She knew teams that do not work together closely have low trust and difficulty dealing with conflict, so she began by improving communications. Her early motto was, "Overcommunicate." She spoke frequently with her managers and encouraged them to talk more with their employ-ees. She also took time to meet with the managers and their employees together to get a sense for what was working and what needed to be improved. In those meetings, she strongly encouraged everyone to begin sharing information so that they could benefit from each other's ideas when addressing depart-mental problems.

She changed the decision-making process in her team because she wanted more consensus and buy-in from the managers, not the kind of submissiveness that the former director had demanded. She wanted active team participation in problem solving, deci-sion making, and ultimately implementation. Fran also worked with HR to develop a reward process that put more recognition on team accomplishments than it did on individual ones. Over time, the cohesiveness of the team clearly improved.

## Emotional Intelligence

We know that conflict involves emotions. In many ways, it is all about emotions. How leaders and members control their team's emotional climate can make the difference between successfully using task conflict or experiencing the downsides of relationship conflict.

Why is emotional intelligence so important in helping teams create the right climate for managing and resolving conflict effectively? For one thing, research has shown that emotionally intelligent teams are more cohesive (Rapisarda, 2002). Teams that exhibit effective emotional awareness and control are able to work more closely and achieve behavioral integration.

Members of emotionally intelligent teams also learn to trust one another more (Prati and others, 2003). It is easier to recognize that colleagues care about you when they show empathy for how you are feeling. The same is true when you show empathy toward them. There are also fewer violations of trust caused by team members who are reacting out of frustration and anger because they are better able to control these emotions.

Emotionally intelligent teams exhibit higher levels of creativity and better performance outcomes (Prati and others, 2003; Feyerherm and Rice, 2002). It is easier for team members to open up and take risks. There is less volatility and less risk in discussing issues when people have differences, thus enabling task conflict to thrive. When team members manage their emotions effectively, they are less likely to lash out at one another, so there is less relationship conflict.

## Emotional Intelligence in Teams

Although there are different understandings of emotional intelligence, the term generally encompasses awareness of one's own emotions, being able to manage them effectively, recognizing other people's emotions, and managing interpersonal relationships that are affected by emotions (Goleman, 1995).

In team contexts, emotional intelligence encompasses these same elements. It also involves the development of team norms that help guide how team members view and interpret emotions in others, which helps keep the overall focus on team priorities instead of interpersonal animosities (Rapisarda, 2002). Teams need to recognize and acknowledge that they will have conflicts, and at times those conflicts will lead to emotional tension. This is natural and inevitable.

Team members need to talk about how they want to respond to emotions. This includes developing norms for when and with whom it is safe to talk about emotions—for example, "We agree that when we experience emotions in the team related to conflict, we will talk openly and honestly with our teammates and not behind their backs." The norm may also address how to express the emotions—for instance, "We agree to talk about how the other person's actions made us feel and not use that as an excuse to attack the other person for the things we think he or she did."

## How Emotions Arise

Our brain scans sensory data and looks for patterns that indicate possible threats. Research psychologist Paul Ekman (2003) calls the parts of the brain that do this *auto-appraisers*. It is like threat radar running underneath our sense of awareness. Certain patterns, like having something thrown at your head, are almost universally recognized as threats and generate rapid responses, like dodging away from the object. We do not think about our response at the moment; it is automatic. Ekman suggests that other patterns differ from one person to another. Individuals learn these patterns early in life based on their individual experiences. Some may learn to view unreliable people as threats because early in life they were let down by others at important times. Others may learn that angry, hostile people are threats because people who exhibited such behaviors harmed them. In later life, these patterns are what the brain's auto-appraisers look to in order to distinguish potential threats.

In conflict settings, our colleagues Sal Capobianco, Mark Davis, and Linda Kraus have termed these patterns *hot buttons*.

Certain situations or behaviors in others cause individuals to become upset and can trigger angry reactions. Table 3.1 shows a list of hot button behaviors related to workplace conflict measured by the Conflict Dynamics Profile assessment instrument (Capobianco, Davis, and Kraus, 2004).

People have widely varying hot button profiles. Some may have only one or two hot button patterns that evoke emotional

### Table 3.1 Hot Buttons

| Hot Button | Your Response |
| --- | --- |
| Unreliable | You get especially irritated and upset when working with people who are unreliable, miss deadlines, and cannot be counted on. |
| Overly Analytical | You get especially irritated and upset when working with people who are perfectionists, overanalyze things, and focus too much on minor issues. |
| Unappreciative | You get especially irritated and upset when working with people who fail to give credit to others or seldom praise good performance. |
| Aloof | You get especially irritated and upset when working with people who isolate themselves, do not seek input from others, or are hard to approach. |
| Micro-Managing | You get especially irritated and upset when working with people who constantly monitor and check up on the work of others. |
| Self-Centered | You get especially irritated and upset when working with people who are self-centered or believe they are always correct. |
| Abrasive | You get especially irritated and upset when working with people who are arrogant, sarcastic, and abrasive. |
| Untrustworthy | You get especially irritated and upset when working with people who exploit others, take undeserved credit, or cannot be trusted. |
| Hostile | You get especially irritated and upset when working with people who lose their tempers, become angry, or yell at others. |

Source: Capobianco, Davis, and Kraus (2004). Used by permission.

responses, while others may have many. If two people view a third individual acting in a particular manner, it would be very possible for one person to get angry while the other remains indifferent. The one whose hot buttons have been pushed views the same behavior as his unaffected colleague does, but he views the behavior as a threat—a threat to his self-esteem, position, or something else. The colleague who saw the same actions by the third individual did not get upset because the pattern did not fit one that she learned to associate with threats.

## The Role of Thinking

When we perceive threats or our hot buttons are triggered, we start to feel emotions. At the same time, we begin to think about the situation. Thinking clearly, though, is a challenge because our mind is clouded by the presence of fear, anger, or other emotions. So as we start thinking, we often have a negative predisposition caused by the emotions that keep us from being objective. We begin creating stories about why other people are acting the way they are. As our colleague Dan Dana (2005) notes, we begin to invent intentions that we ascribe to others, although in truth we do not know what they are thinking. The process becomes exaggerated when we have previously had negative experiences with the others. When we have a history with them, we leap to negative conclusions based on prior experiences and rapidly attribute dark motives to their actions. As these thoughts emerge, they fan our emotional flames. If we feel angry at other people and begin to think about their actions, we usually become convinced that our anger is justified by their bad actions and intentions, which makes us angrier still. This heightened anger makes it even harder to think clearly and easier to believe that a retaliatory action is justified (Allred, 2000).

Different parts of our brain are involved in these functions. Emotions are triggered in the amygdala. The part of the brain involved with modulating emotions is the prefrontal cortex.

Recent advances in brain research have discovered an interesting phenomenon: when people are experiencing negative emotions like fear or anger, the amygdala and the right prefrontal cortex are active. So when you are upset with someone because of a conflict, those are the active portions of your brain. Interestingly, when people feel positive emotions like happiness or compassion, the amygdala and the left prefrontal cortex are active. This fact plays a key role in the techniques for controlling emotions. Later in this chapter, we look at a variety of disciplines that help control both mental and physical states, which in turn affect your emotional states.

One more interesting fact is worth sharing at this point: when the emotional stresses associated with conflict reach a certain point, specific hormones are released that get the body ready for fight-or-flight responses. These hormones also affect our brain and reduce our cognitive ability, which makes rational thinking very difficult. While this can be important in life-threatening contexts (you do not want to be having extended internal debates when immediate action is required), it can make dealing with conflict in ordinary team settings more difficult.

## How Emotions Spread

If emotions affected only the individuals involved in a conflict, they would be difficult enough. But they are even more challenging in teams because they can spread from one person to others. We know that people in conflict talk to colleagues, who might take sides and develop their own emotional attachments to the problem. The process is even subtler than this, though. In his book *Social Intelligence* (2007a), Daniel Goleman describes the process of emotional contagion, which occurs very rapidly outside our normal awareness It is akin to empathy but occurs silently and automatically. Goleman likens it to a feedback loop where one person's emotions are picked up on by others in a group, who do more than just recognize that another person is experiencing it. They begin to feel the same emotion themselves. Specific brain cells called mirror neurons enable us to see the emotion on someone else's face and begin to sense the same emotions ourselves (Hotz, 2007). Once this happens, our brains also prepare us to act on the emotions as well. So Goleman suggests that it is important for teams to be aware of emotions in the room, as well as what other people are saying. Since emotions can spread so rapidly, they can have a significant effect not only on individuals but on the climate of the whole team.

## Controlling Your Emotions

It is clear that negative thoughts and emotions can make it difficult to think clearly and deal effectively with conflict. Learning how to control these emotions so that they do not get the best of you and cause inevitable differences to become heightened conflicts is important.

### Understanding Your Emotional Triggers

You can learn to understand what triggers your negative emotions in the first place and then develop strategies to keep those triggers from causing you to get off balance and respond destructively.

*Becoming Aware of What Triggers You.* We often have clients take the Conflict Dynamics Profile assessment instrument, in part to help them look at what triggers their hot buttons. By recognizing the behaviors that upset you, you can learn to anticipate when you will be in situations where people engage in those behaviors. If you do not have access to an assessment instrument, you can still think about what types of behaviors in others cause you to get angry in the first place. We suggest making a list of those behaviors or circumstances, so that you can reflect on why they cause you so much difficulty.

**Cooling Down.** Once you understand the behaviors that can push your hot buttons, begin to look at ways to keep them from getting out of control. There are a number of processes to help cool down your reactions to hot buttons or perceived threats. Many people recommend taking some deep breaths. Another suggestion is to think of something pleasant to distract your attention from the conflict. Others advise viewing the situation through a different lens to see it in a less threatening light. Underlying these common suggestions are several more refined techniques that can make a significant difference in the way that you respond emotionally to conflict. They come from disciplines that focus on developing control over the body and mind.

**Breathing and Centering.** In the martial arts, a great deal of attention is paid to being able to center oneself physically and emotionally. One of our colleagues, Judy Ringer, a master in the martial art of aikido, describes a process of physically bringing the body into a balanced state. For practice, she has you stand and feel whether your body is off balance. She then directs you to focus on your center of gravity slightly below the navel, while beginning to take deep breaths to help calm you and center your attention further (Ringer, 2006).

When you use these techniques, you instantly feel calmer and more balanced in both your body and your mind. These processes help the martial artist prepare to engage an attacker, but they also help anyone in conflict prepare to engage the other person in a more effective manner. The process takes away the desire to run away or lash out and encourages constructive engagement with the other person.

**Observing Your Thoughts and Feelings.** Common wisdom suggests thinking of something positive to distract your attention away from negative thoughts and emotions. This has merit, but it is difficult to stay focused when you are upset. Although you may be able to think of something pleasant for a moment, it is hard to keep from returning to the distressing thoughts and emotions occasioned by the conflict. Other approaches serve a similar function and can be more effective.

One technique is the process of reflecting: taking note of your own thoughts and emotions so that you can review them with a sense of skepticism. By stopping to observe your own thinking and the feelings associated with the thoughts, you will find that the emotions begin to lose their power over you. In effect, you can ask yourself, "How am I interpreting the situation such that I am reacting in this way?" (Edmondson and Smith, 2006, p. 14).

A similar concept is the practice of mindfulness—an awareness that comes from paying attention, in the present moment, to your experiences. As you become aware of your thoughts as they are unfolding, you stop judging what is happening and instead merely observe it (Gunaratana, 2002). This can be difficult because you feel so much a part of the conflict and identify yourself with the thoughts and feelings you are experiencing. When you can step back and distance your sense of self from the troubling thoughts and emotions, they soon begin to lose their hold over you (Siegel, 2007). There is a difference between who you are and what you are thinking and feeling, and by being mindful and observant, this distinction becomes apparent. It also enables you to see things more clearly and be fully present mentally so that you can attend more effectively to the conflict (Gerzon, 2006; Tolle, 2004).

Another interesting thing happens when you are able to slow down and observe your own thoughts: changes occur in your brain function. As you will recall, when people are in the grip of destructive emotions, the amygdala and right prefrontal cortex become active. When people are able to observe their thoughts and feelings—when they are being mindful—the brain pattern shifts. The amygdala is still involved, but the activity switches from the right to the left prefrontal cortex. Mindfulness activates the left prefrontal area. In effect, there is a change from a pattern associated with destructive emotions to one that is related to positive ones (Siegel, 2007).

A variation on this approach is to withdraw your attention from the destructive thoughts and feelings and focus on something more personally inspiring to you. It is more than just trying to think of something pleasant to distract your mind. Rather, it involves being aware of what is occurring and then consciously replacing the negative thoughts with ones that are inspiring to you (personal communication, yogic monk A. Y. Avadhuta to C.E.R., 2007). The approaches of being mindful and consciously substituting uplifting thoughts in place of negative ones represent mental techniques derived from two ancient approaches to contemplative or meditative practice (Goleman and Dass, 1987).

These disciplines of the mind have particular applicability in helping people deal more effectively with emotions that are thrown out of control by the inevitable conflicts that we experience in our lives. These mental techniques typically involve learning how to increase your ability to concentrate, cultivate an awareness of how you subjectively see issues, and sharpen your ability to reflect on and de-emphasize this subjectivity (Siegel, 2007).

Honing these abilities through mental practice can help lessen emotional tensions during conflict and even prevent emotions from getting out of control in the first place. Research conducted by Richard Davidson and colleagues at the University of Wisconsin has shown that meditative practices may strengthen people's ability to lessen or prevent negative emotions from gaining the upper hand in the first place. It appears that these techniques can create positive moods in individuals, which may serve as antidotes to negative emotions that can arise when hot buttons are pushed. They may also lower the degree to which we ruminate on issues and thus escalate emotional tension by thinking destructive thoughts about the situation (Brefczynski-Lewis and others, 2007; Siegel, 2007). And they may contribute to our resilience, or ability to bounce back from negative emotions. Although these practices may appear difficult, research suggests that they are quite achievable (Goleman, 2003; Davidson and others, 2003).

**Getting Back in Balance.** In conflict contexts, we suggest using these techniques to cool down. Otherwise it is easy to get pulled into a cascade of negative thoughts and feelings that make it extremely difficult to manage conflict effectively. If you can step back and become aware of what is happening, you will become more balanced and deal with conflict more effectively.

Once our emotions are back in balance and we have calmed down, it becomes easier to reframe the situation from an adversarial context to one where all parties have legitimate concerns. A calmer state of mind enables us to recognize ways in which we may have contributed to the conflict. It also helps us feel more empathy with the other person. Psychologist Paul Ekman suggests that there are varying levels of empathy. The level of cognitive empathy means trying to understand where the others are coming from without necessarily sympathizing with them. A second level is emotional empathy, where you are actually feeling what the other person feels. The final type is compassionate empathy, when you have both a cognitive and emotional understanding of the other and some care and concern about that person's welfare (Goleman, 2007b). Our brains appear to have a built-in capacity for this compassion or willingness to care about others (Goleman, 2007a). It seems that in order for this to be active, the mind needs to be calm. Controlling emotions gives you access to compassionate capabilities that are lacking when you are feeling destructive emotions. When you can become attuned to the other person, this empathy often helps them calm down as well. The sense of feeling that someone else understands and cares not only lessens tension but also helps build trust. At that point, a conflict opponent can become a conflict partner. We become able to think about the conflict from many sides in a process called reflective thinking. And we are able to consider novel approaches for creating solutions where both parties can gain (Capobianco, Davis, and Kraus, 2004; Siegal, 2007).

## Reappraising What's Happening

We have discussed the problems with attribution. We often think that others' motives are worse than they actually are, and this causes us to feel threatened and get upset. Looking at the situation to find less sinister motives can dampen your emotions. This process is referred to as reframing; that is, you consider the situation from new frames of reference. It is associated with a psychological concept called cognitive reappraisal, described by a quote from Marcus Aurelius: "If you are distressed by anything external, the pain is not due to the thing itself, but to your estimate of it; and this you have the power to revoke at any moment."

Cognitive reappraisal means reinterpreting the meaning of what you see or hear. You may initially construe another person's actions as hostile to your interests. Perhaps you think they are moving in on your turf or trying to make you look bad in front of others. Although this is certainly possible, there may be innocent reasons for their actions. Research has shown that reappraising situations can lessen emotional tension. In particular, changes in brain activity are analogous to those that occur when a person uses reflection and mindfulness techniques (Ochsner and Gross, 2005; Ray and others, 2005; Ochsner, Bunge, Gross, and Gabrieli, 2002). When this happens, negative emotions lessen and more positive emotions emerge.

## Cooling Things Down in the Team

These insights into emotional self-control and developing empathy for others are important in helping manage relationships within a team, particularly when conflict has moved from task to relationship conflict. The reasons that relationship conflict emerges are often related to the team's emotional climate. Dealing effectively with conflict requires being aware of emotions as they arise. It is easier when you catch them early, before they have escalated. In Chapter Four, we discuss perspective taking, which you can use to understand how others are thinking and feeling. It can help keep conflict focused on task issues and prevent it from turning into relationship conflict. It can also aid in addressing relationship conflict when it does emerge, so that it does not escalate and cause serious problems for the team.

Another approach to dealing with emotional issues within a team setting looks at people's general concerns more than at emotions themselves. This approach, developed by Roger Fisher and Dan Shapiro at Harvard University, discusses managing core concerns that all people share, thereby preventing negative emotional responses in the first place. In their book *Beyond Reason* (2005), Fisher and Shapiro identify five core concerns: appreciation, affiliation, autonomy, status, and role concerns. Appreciation is acknowledging the value of other people on your team. Affiliation deals with developing closer connections with team members. Affiliation amounts to improving behavioral integration in the team, working more closely with one another. Autonomy means respecting the freedom of others to make their own decisions. In team conflicts, this could be expanded to include respecting the right of people to see matters differently. It acknowledges the value of diversity and the rights of people to pursue decisions that they believe are correct. This has to be balanced against the importance of deciding issues that are of value to the team as well as to individual members. The fourth core concern is status: recognizing that each person has special skills, talents, and capacities. In a cross-functional team, this may include acknowledging the different educational backgrounds and experiences that each person brings to the team. The final core concern is role, which relates to making sure that people have a clear, meaningful sense of purpose. In a team, this includes clarifying team members' responsibilities and recognizing the importance of each person's unique contribution to team success.

The benefit of the Fisher-Shapiro model is that it focuses on a set of easily understood concerns that all people have, which allows teams to make sure that these concerns are addressed for all team members. When they are, there is less chance that negative emotions will arise and turn conflict into something destructive. Fisher and Shapiro recognize that addressing core concerns will not always keep negative emotions from rising and suggest having backup plans for when they do.

We also recommend having a backup plan. In our case, it is a plan for slowing down when your efforts at controlling emotions do not seem to be working. Dealing with emotions is difficult. Even when you have addressed core concerns, it is possible for negative emotions to arise. This can result in destructive responses that move conflict away from a task focus to one that deals with personalities and relationships. In these cases, things can spin out of control quickly, and people can inflict harm on one another.

## Slowing Down

When you find yourself, despite your best efforts, getting off balance and about to say or do something you may later regret, it is time to stop. These situations often arise quickly, and you can find yourself losing control in the heat of the moment. For this reason, it is important to map out a fallback plan before conflict occurs. You may think of a number of ways of being able to call a time-out to allow time for emotions to calm down so you can use the techniques described earlier in this chapter. Depending on the circumstances, you may be able to ask for a restroom break, a coffee break, or some other kind of break. In other situations, it may be worthwhile to tell the other people that you are getting angry and do not want to respond at this point. Let them know that you need to take a few moments to calm down so that you can discuss the issue in the careful manner that it deserves.

It is prudent to have several backup strategies to address different contexts. The key is for you to have some plans in mind that you can use when the situation is beginning to spin out of control. This is not the time to expect clear thinking, and you need to have a plan that you can automatically call on to enable you to buy some time to get back in control. Once you cool down and reflect on what is happening, you can consider alternative ways of looking at the situation and be prepared to resume discussions from a more constructive vantage point.

## What to Do When Things Are Stuck

Sometimes teams get stuck in a pattern where things will be calm for a while and then dysfunctions reappear. When this pattern emerges, there may be festering hidden issues. They may lay dormant for a time, but they almost certainly will recur. In these situations, it is necessary to look for hidden conflicts (Lencioni, 2005). Our colleague Michael Kossler, from the Center for Creative Leadership, worked with a senior team in the health care field that was experiencing this type of situation.

The team was composed of very talented individuals who had been working together for a long time, but they experienced recurrent issues that kept them from performing as well as they wanted. Michael was called in to help the team find a solution to their communication problems. In this case he used a technique called "emptying the gunny sack." He had each of the team members spend a short time talking one-on-one with every other team member. They shared any prior issues they had with the other person. After a complete round, they discovered a collection of simmering emotional issues that had gone unspoken. These issues made it hard for certain team members even to listen to others. Their history was getting in the way. After detecting these hidden issues, the team took time to discuss them, and team members began to be able to let go of them. They were finally able to start listening to one another again. We provide additional approaches for teams that are stuck in Chapter Five.

## The Role of the Team Leader

Team leaders can have a profound impact on the emotional climate of their teams. It is particularly important for them to demonstrate emotional control and show positive moods themselves. They need to be sensitive and empathetic toward other team members' emotional states. Finally, they need to avoid behaving in ways that would cause distress to others and address situations where feelings have been hurt.

Leaders who demonstrate positive moods and effective emotional control can create a positive climate within their teams. When a leader conveys news, her tone and demeanor may have greater impact than the content of the message (Goleman, 2007a). Upbeat leaders generate more positive responses from team members than do moody or grouchy ones, so team leaders need to work on their own emotional self-control as a starting point.

It is important for team leaders to take the emotional temperature of team members, especially when conflict is occurring. They need to help team members openly express their concerns. When the intensity of the discussion becomes too high, they need to guard against negative emotions taking control. They can do this by calling for a break and checking with team members to see how they are feeling and encouraging them to share their feelings with others. Leaders should be attentive to looks, body language, and behaviors that belie otherwise positive comments. They can also help the team develop a norm where they agree to share their feelings and discuss issues early, before emotions get out of control.

Leaders need to show empathy and concern toward others. They must avoid using destructive behaviors that would cause team members to get upset. Research has shown that leaders' use of demeaning behaviors can have a profound negative impact on employees, causing them to withdraw or respond destructively to team initiatives (Goleman, 2007a).

Executive coach Joe Tomaselli tells of a time when such behaviors almost cost a team leader his job. The team leader was technically brilliant but had poor people management skills and frequently responded to conflict by using hostile, demeaning language. Team members responded in kind, and everyone was looking for ways to score points at others' expense. As Joe noted, the team was playing a game of "gotcha." The leader's behaviors were setting the wrong tone and were leading to destructive responses by other team members. Joe worked with the leader to help him understand the need to stop acting destructively. They worked on eliminating the blame game and focused on developing shared responsibility within the team. In time, the atmosphere began to turn for the better.

You may have seen or experienced similar situations where leaders were behaving poorly and poisoning the team environment. We suggest that this approach virtually guarantees that teams will get the worst out of conflict. Leaders need to set a good example if they want the team to deal with conflict effectively.

A leader who makes a mistake and hurts someone or sees that others have acted in a similar manner needs to move quickly to address the situation and make efforts to repair the harm. Emotions that are allowed to fester can easily escalate to a point where rational discussion is no longer possible and team progress is thwarted. Wise leaders address emotional harm quickly.

Fran was aware of behaviors that upset her and knew it would be a challenge to deal with a couple of her managers. She recognized that both she and the other members of her team would need help in being able to deal with their emotions more effectively. In the previous environment, the only sensible course of action was to suppress one's feelings. Fran knew that this was not an effective approach and asked the consultant who conducted the team-building exercises to also work with her group to improve their emotional intelligence. Through the use of assessment instruments and exercises, the team began to recognize areas where they were effective and others where they were going to need to improve.

## Team Member Support

The team leader plays a critical role, but all members of the team have to work together to address conflict effectively. They need to participate in developing and upholding team norms, which support and empower individual team members to step in when they see relationship conflict emerging that can harm the team. A team member who sees other teammates acting in ways that are breaching trust or contributing to destructive conflict can intercede and remind the others of the team norms for how to deal with conflict. If one team member comes to another to seek advice about how to handle a conflict, the person should feel free to give it and refer back to the team norms in doing so.

## Starting Out Right

Most of the focus in this chapter has been on existing teams. So what should a team leader have in mind when creating a new team? Certainly the leader will want team members who have the right skills and experience to address the issues for which the team is being formed. Although this is important, the leader should also make sure that the team is one whose members will be able to get along with one another and will be able to deal with conflict effectively. If they are not able to do this, the team will have considerable difficulty accomplishing its goals, regardless of the degree of talent. This is why so many apparent dream teams fail (Colvin, 2006).

Teams can benefit from having members with different educational and functional backgrounds. When team members bring diverse sets of information to the team, it can be used to bring out new ideas and make task conflict effective (Homan, van Knippenberg, Van Kleef, and De Dreu, 2007a). While informational diversity can help teams, value differences can cause problems. As we have noted, conflicts over values can be difficult to manage and often turn into relationship conflict. Most research confirms that value differences among team members can prove problematic (Jehn, Chadwick, and Thatcher, 1997). Additional problems can emerge when members fall into subgroups that may create an us-versus-them stance on the team. So a leader should avoid purposely building a team whose members might have such an attitude. If this is not possible, then the leader must work with team members from the outset to emphasize the value that diversity brings to the team (Homan, van Knippenberg, Van Kleef, and De Dreu, 2007b).

One effective approach for a team leader is to find people who have worked well together in the past (Gratton and Erickson, 2007). Although this will not prevent conflict, it suggests that the people have skills that will enable them to find ways to work through it successfully. The team will still have to develop operating norms, but they have a greater likelihood of following them if they have done it in the past.

## Once the Climate Is Right

In this chapter, we have looked at elements that create the right climate to enable teams to deal effectively with conflict. By adjusting attitudes toward conflict, building trust and safety, working collaboratively, and developing emotional intelligence, teams can create a climate where members can openly discuss issues, debate vigorously, and constructively criticize others' approaches. Setting the right climate is one step in building a conflict competent team. Team members still have to communicate effectively with one another. They need to use behaviors and techniques that are calculated to help them get the best out of conflict. When the climate is right, communications will be easier, but they cannot be taken for granted. In the next two chapters, we explore how teams can manage this complex process.

## Components for Building Conflict Competent Teams

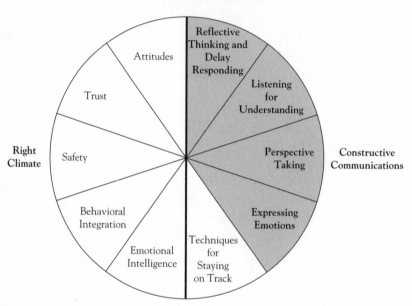

# 4

# CONSTRUCTIVE COMMUNICATION

> The biggest problem with communication is the
> illusion that it has been accomplished.
>
> —*George Bernard Shaw*

Interpersonal communication is perhaps the single most analyzed, most researched, and most investigated topic in the field of training and development. In our many years of experience in the field, we wouldn't hesitate to say that the vast majority of the leadership and team development training classes we've presented or attended have addressed interpersonal communication. So it feels a bit obvious to suggest that constructive communication is one of the core characteristics of conflict competent teams. It's just not a major revelation. The rather sobering truth of the matter is that if teams and team members communicate constructively on a consistent basis, there would be a lot less destructive conflict in teams, and we would be writing a different book.

Patrick Lencioni (2002) describes the interaction of an *absence of trust* and a *fear of conflict* as the first two of his five dysfunctions of a team. He suggests that teams suffering from these two dysfunctions are essentially devoid of open, honest communication. Eloquently and simply he suggests that these teams are "incapable of engaging in unfiltered and passionate debate of ideas" (p. 188). This lack of candor stifles creativity and innovation, as well as a team's ability to effectively address the conflict. This inability to communicate openly, honestly, and completely jeopardizes the very essence of a team's potential. Furthermore, lacking constructive communication, team members may then succumb to destructive behaviors, including guarded discussions, attributions, anger, avoidance, and sometimes fruitless gossip about fellow team members. As the conflict spirals out of control, the team suffers not only from lack of productivity, but damage to the team climate and lack of collaboration. Perhaps one more chapter focusing on constructive communication in another book isn't such a bad idea after all.

## Intra-Team Versus Inter-Team Conflict

Our work is focused almost exclusively on conflicts between and among team members on the same team: intra-team conflict. Of course, there are times when conflict emerges between teams. We suggest that these inter-team conflicts can be addressed in many of the same ways two individuals address conflict. The constructive behaviors and skills that individuals use can help teams cool down, slow down, and reengage when conflict emerges between teams. The implications of inter-team conflict on the organization may be more complex than the impact of intra-team conflict. This topic is certainly worthy of much more attention than we are giving it here. We wish to be clear: our intent throughout this book is to focus on constructively handling conflict within teams.

## The Human Condition

Let's face it: we are prisoners of our own condition. As human beings, we are stuck with our five senses. If we can see it, touch it, smell it, hear it, or taste it, we can usually make some sense of it. When communicating with our fellow human beings, we use the same five senses and a language. When there is a shared knowledge of the language, communication is generally understandable. Even when we speak different languages, some understanding is usually possible if all parties make an effort. Can you recall a time when you tried to communicate with someone speaking a language different from yours? Concentrating on gestures, speaking slowly, and drawing symbols probably helped the communication process. Most important, we suspect that you were intently focused on making the communication work. In other words, you and your partner were genuinely trying to understand each other. Regrettably, in today's world where information is available in overwhelming quantities and with incredible speed, we often assume clarity and understanding, especially when speaking the same language. The question is, How can we overcome our tendency to assume that we are communicating clearly?

And there's more. An additional human condition contributes to both the potential depth of our communication and the potential for misunderstanding: our emotionality. As we discussed in Chapter Three, we are emotional beings. Our emotions provide color, depth, and spirit to our lives, and they can greatly enhance our ability to communicate and connect with one another. But those same emotions provide a fragile, complex, and sometimes volatile basis for misunderstanding. When we mix our propensity for misunderstandings with emotions, we have a tried-and-true recipe for conflict. It also stands to reason that the greater the number of people involved in communicating, such as in teams, the greater the likelihood is for misunderstandings and conflict. The greater the volume of information (words, tone, and nonverbals, for example) communicated and the more filters (people) the information passes through, the greater the potential is for misinterpretation. Remember the game of telephone, where one person whispers a message to the next person in a circle, then that person whispers the same message to another, until everyone has heard it? The original message is almost never the same as the final message. The question now becomes, How can we overcome our tendencies to assume that we are communicating clearly, especially in teams or groups, while dealing with emotions effectively?

For all the potential pitfalls associated with miscommunicating, constructive communication is the key to handling conflict in teams. Without the ability to communicate, it is impossible to establish and maintain the right climate or achieve complete collaboration. We want to be clear: constructive communication is not a substitute for establishing and maintaining the right climate. Neither can exist without the other. Teams must reduce the harmful effects of poor or destructive communication and instead practice constructive communication. The way we engage, speak, listen, hear, interpret, and respond leads directly to understanding or misunderstanding our differences. This is at the very foundation of all conflicts. And because we have the power to choose how we engage, speak, listen, hear, interpret, and respond, we are in control of shaping the results of our differences and the outcomes of our conflicts. In teams, we must exercise choices that enhance our opportunities to leverage conflict constructively rather than make choices that exacerbate the harmful aspects of conflict.

## Intensity

Another complicating factor in our challenge to communicate clearly before, during, and after conflict is associated with the intensity level of the current conflict. As we described in *Becoming a Conflict Competent Leader* (Runde and Flanagan, 2007), the intensity of conflict can escalate rapidly. In order to emphasize this concept, we compared the intensity levels of conflict to the scale used to describe the five intensity levels of hurricanes. Just as we associate different ways to prepare for and recover from storms of various strengths or intensity, we believe it's valuable to consider the intensity levels of our conflicts as a factor in shaping our responses:

Level 1: Differences

Level 2: Misunderstandings

Level 3: Disagreements

Level 4: Discord

Level 5: Polarization

Many of us may not even notice the early levels of conflict as problematic. It's only when the conflict becomes moderately or highly intense that we recognize that we are dealing with a conflict. Similarly, and unfortunately, many residents of the hurricane belt pay little attention to level 1 or 2 storms. They wait until the hurricane has strengthened to major proportions before making crucial decisions, a practice that can result in catastrophe. Though conflicts are never catastrophic on the same scale, once a conflict reaches the more intense levels, it is considerably more challenging to resolve.

## Differences

Level 1 of intensity is Differences. We define this level as when two or more people see a situation differently, understand the other parties' positions and interests well, and feel no discomfort regarding the difference.

Earlier in my career, I (Tim) was a member of a team of instructors working at the corporate training center for the Harris Corporation. We were in the midst of a project to update our facilities. During one of our planning meetings, we invited a vendor to demonstrate some of its newest state-of-the-art equipment. Our team was very impressed with the newest projection system, which would allow us to use a single large screen in each classroom. During the demonstration, we began discussing the purchase and potential uses of this new technology.

Don suggested that we buy one unit. He thought the best location for the new system was our largest classroom, because it's where we were getting most of the complaints regarding difficulty viewing the television monitors. Stan thought that we should consider purchasing multiple systems for all of our main classrooms. If we didn't, he reasoned, participants in the smaller classrooms would complain about the older technology. Nancy, one of our contract instructors, was concerned that the new equipment might not work with our existing video replay equipment. Unless we were certain that it would work with our current systems, she suggested we not move ahead with the purchase. Russ, our boss, shared with us that we had funds in our budget to equip several classrooms. He also said that he had read about an even better projector that had just hit the market. I was impressed with the demonstration but wanted to explore more options.

In summary, each of the five team members had a different idea about how to proceed. Don and I admitted that we had not thought that equipping just one classroom could lead to more complaints from those in our smaller classrooms with lower-quality equipment (Stan had). Russ thought it was a good idea to make sure our existing equipment was compatible with the new equipment (Nancy's point). All of us were interested in learning about the next new technology (Russ's view). We each saw the situation differently. More important, we were happy to listen to all of the views and discuss them. There was no animosity, no discomfort about our differences. In fact, our differences ultimately led to a richer, deeper debate about our needs. We decided to investigate several other systems and found a vendor that provided upgrades when new technology was invented and gave a large-volume discount for equipping multiple classrooms. Ultimately the team and the organization benefited from the differences among the team members.

Most of us probably don't consider differences to be a form of conflict. We suggest that differences contain the very essence of healthy conflict. When teams can deal with conflict while it's low in intensity, conflict becomes an asset.

## Misunderstandings

Level 2 of intensity is Misunderstandings, that is, times or situations when what is understood by one party is different from what is understood by other parties. Misunderstandings are commonplace. In most cases, they are relatively inconsequential blips in life that are discovered and handled rather easily. In many cases, we barely remember that there was any confusion or misunderstanding at all. We take care of it and move on.

The difficulty arises when misunderstandings cause problems or issues that take time to resolve. The tension rises when misunderstandings result in somebody being inconvenienced or embarrassed. And things can really get interesting when misunderstandings lead to missed targets, opportunities, appointments, commitments, and obligations. Attributions begin forming, accusations may follow, and before you know it, you have a full-fledged ugly conflict of a destructive nature on your hands.

We identify misunderstandings as the second level of intensity because we believe they are a bit unpredictable. How often have you heard somebody explain an error on an invoice as an "honest" misunderstanding or being late for a lunch meeting as a "friendly" misunderstanding? These kinds of misunderstanding are like puppies: they sort of bounce up to greet you with tail wagging and tongue licking. There is no problem with honest or friendly misunderstandings. Like encountering puppies, we usually smile, laugh, and continue. But some puppies grow up to be fierce jaw-snapping mongrels we avoid at all costs. Some misunderstandings grow into difficult conflicts.

In teams, we like to believe that all misunderstandings start out as the honest or friendly variety. We prefer to assume positive intent. Because misunderstandings can be ironed out easily most of the time, the intensity seldom rises to high levels. Of course, the longer a misunderstanding goes unresolved, the greater the likelihood is that it will grow to higher intensity levels. And the more critical the misunderstood issue is to the team, the more potential there is for intensity escalation. The greatest caution when it comes to teams is that misunderstandings reach out to envelop more than one person. Each team member may have a slightly different view of the misunderstanding and therefore be affected in different ways. A once seemingly friendly or honest misunderstanding suddenly grows into a complex, cavernous conflict.

Frequent misunderstandings may be a symptom of other issues connected not only with poor communication but with the team climate or team agreements. When the frequency of misunderstanding is high, team members must take special care to ensure shared understanding at all times. This means slowing down the communication, checking for understanding frequently, and summarizing all agreements. We'll discuss a number of techniques and skills later in this chapter.

## Disagreements

Level 3 of intensity is Disagreements. We think of disagreements as times when two or more people see a situation differently and, regardless of how well they understand the other positions and interests, they feel discomfort that the other parties disagree. This is the midpoint of the intensity scale and in many ways illustrates the delicate fulcrum of conflict. At the Disagreements level, conflict can move quickly from constructive to destructive, friendly to adversarial, productive to ineffective. This happens for several reasons. First, disagreements by their very nature touch our emotions. Once emotions are aroused in a conflict, the more difficult it becomes to overcome them. Second, disagreements on a team affect every team member. Complexity grows as each member wrangles with the issue, and, of course, one disagreement can lead to another. When a pattern of disagreement appears on a team, resolution becomes the most important task for it. Disagreement undermines the team's ability to achieve its goals because it takes the focus off the team's mission and purpose. In other words, attention becomes more focused on relationship than on task.

A disagreement may not be a terrible thing in and of itself. It can be a signal to a team to slow down and examine underlying differences that may hold the key to new ideas or creative solutions or to revisit team agreements or team mission. More than anything else, a disagreement means that there are at least two different views held by team members who have an investment in those views. We suggest that at moments like this, both or all views should be fully considered. Certainly teams can expect to encounter disagreements from time to time. Those that have established the right climate and engage in constructive communication regarding the disagreement will be poised to take advantage of the conflict, or at least work through it confidently.

A team that experiences disagreement on an important topic potentially will have to navigate a variety of hazardous twists and turns. When traveling on the disagreement highway, excessive speed, lack of attention, disregard for safety, or poor judgment can cause a serious crash. And successfully handling those same twists and turns can result in a very satisfying trip.

Carl Larson and Frank LaFasto published *Teamwork: What Must Go Right/What Can Go Wrong* in 1989. The book was the result of a research project designed to develop a system for monitoring the effectiveness of teams and provide feedback to them. As they gathered data, they heard incredible stories from team members that reflected a number of consistent themes about the highest-performing teams, and their project evolved into a groundbreaking description of what it takes for a team to be effective. One of the more memorable examples from their research illustrates the sometimes delicate balance among team members that once upset can lead to a disagreement of major proportions.

A seventeen-member research team was sent to Antarctica on a scientific expedition. In order to conserve fuel, team members were permitted to bathe once every seventeen days. The process of bathing had several steps: digging snow, melting it, heating it, and then filling a tub with the warm water. The bather would immediately get into the tub, wash, and then dump his or her dirty laundry into the warm, soapy water. The dirty laundry would get "done" by stepping on it, rinsing it, and then hanging it to dry.

During the course of the expedition, one team member began knocking on the bathroom door every evening asking the bather for a favor. "Could you do this pair of socks for me?" Or, "I spilled coffee on a shirt today. Can you rinse it for me?" In time, the sixteen other members discovered the selfish behavior of their colleague. The ensuing confrontation and disagreement over how to resolve the situation was cited by most team members as the key reason the team ended the expedition early and returned to the mainland.

As illustrated in this example, disagreements handled ineffectively can ultimately lead to the demise of the team. Teams that are able to address disagreements effectively reduce the intensity of the conflict and often discover novel, satisfying outcomes.

## Discord

This fourth level of intensity is a sign that the team is in some difficulty. If an unresolved disagreement has the potential to become the focus of the team, then Discord is the level where that potential is fully realized. When in Discord, the team likely spends a significant portion of time focusing on the conflict rather than their primary purpose or task. Discord is characterized by generally deteriorating relationships among the members in conflict. The team members feel the strain even when they are not dealing with the root issue. It's pervasive in their relationships. We define Discord as situations where the conflict causes difficulties in the relationship of the people involved even when those people are not dealing with the original conflict.

Once a conflict reaches the level of Discord, serious damage to the team's climate and team members' relationships can result if the conflict is not addressed effectively. The parties begin to experience consistent ongoing difficulties with their interactions. When one teammate begins to respond to other teammates by avoiding, criticizing, yielding, demeaning, blocking, scheming, or sabotaging, it is clear that the team climate is suffering and all parties are experiencing discomfort.

For weeks Jason, Dawn, Amber, Laura, John, and Toby had been reeling from their disastrous team presentation to the executive board. The excellent progress report they had hoped to share turned into a nightmare. Depending on who was describing the events, each team member placed blame on another team member. Jason forgot to make copies of the updated report. Dawn didn't load the correct presentation on the laptop. Amber was late for the meeting. Laura and John gave conflicting information during the presentation. And Toby spent fifteen minutes on the summary, so no time was left for questions. Clearly the presentation could have gone better. But rather than focusing on the content of the issues, the team found themselves blaming one another. As the blame game spiraled out of control, teammates found themselves avoiding one another, criticizing each other, and talking behind backs. That was just at work. Outside the office, they had often socialized together. Now they barely spoke as they trudged through the parking lot toward their cars at the end of the day.

Discord can signal the end of a team's ability to perform effectively. In the short term, there's little chance that the team will prosper. Discord can be overcome, but not by avoiding, blaming, criticizing and lashing out. Discord results from differences, misunderstandings, or disagreements that have been mishandled. Teams must engage in dialogue to have any chance of resolving the conflict. Through communication, the team can move the conflict back down the intensity scale. Once cooled down, the conflict can be addressed and resolved. Lessons can be learned and applied. The team can work together again, confident in their experience of overcoming adversity.

If you believe your team is in Discord, it's imperative to address it. Discord unaddressed and unresolved is destined to lead to the final level of intensity, Polarization.

## Polarization

In our discussions with team members who have found themselves at this most intense level of conflict, three common themes seem to be present: the apparent inability or unwillingness of one party to try to see the other party's side of the story, the active recruitment of others for supporting one's position, and differences between the parties so severe that accusations, attributions, and even outbursts become common. Finding a way to work toward some sort of resolution seems futile, and may be impossible.

Our research led us to very few teams that we would categorize at this level. We surmise that teams that reach such destructive levels simply stop functioning. Most are probably disbanded and members given new assignments. If we think of a marriage at the Polarization level, we would expect the couple to be involved in divorce proceedings. If we think of countries at this level, we would describe them as being on the brink of war.

Team members on any team experiencing this level of conflict intensity are suffering. The team itself is suffering. For all intents and purposes, the team is no longer a team. It's simply a group of coworkers who find themselves wondering what went wrong. This level of intensity is damaging, but it is not incurable. The key ingredient, the one absolutely necessary step for there to be any progress, is communication. The team members must agree to talk, they must agree to listen, and they must agree to seek understanding of their teammates' perspectives.

In most cases, a third-party facilitator or expert is appropriate. At the Polarization level, the team's climate contains little or no safety and therefore little or no incentive for team members to be open or vulnerable. A third-party facilitator can provide process and structure that enable the potential for open communication. Individual coaching for team leaders and members may be another viable consideration. Nothing about the recovery from this most intense level is easy. Through constructive communication, though, there is hope.

Understanding the intensity of team conflicts can enable team members to effectively engage in communicating about the conflict. The lower intensities are the easiest to overlook. The higher intensities are impossible to ignore. In between the extremes are vast opportunities to explore the potential of conflict and address disagreements, discord, and misunderstandings constructively.

## Constructive Behaviors and Skills

Because the fundamental building blocks of teams are individuals, we believe it is critical to identify and explore some of the basic individual skills and behaviors that enable constructive engagement of conflict. In the final analysis, it's up to individual team members to develop personal skills and exhibit constructive behaviors toward teammates for conflict to be handled effectively. In much the same way that baseball is a team sport with teams of talented individuals, organizational teams rely on the talent and skill of their players to achieve success. A certain amount of the success of any team depends on the players' capabilities.

It's also imperative that team leaders use constructive communication behaviors and skills effectively. Fair or not, there is an additional burden on team leaders to model the right way to interact. Team members look to their leaders for guidance, coaching, support, and advice. Team leaders who practice constructive communication are likely much more approachable and in a better position to provide feedback, suggest alternatives, and recommend resources to team members. Throughout this book, we address communication behaviors, skills, and techniques for use by all team members. At the same time, we embrace the fact that effective team leaders are held to a higher standard than team members. Whenever we discuss constructive behaviors for team members, we include team leaders.

Capobianco, Davis, and Kraus (2004) identified seven constructive behaviors in their groundbreaking research that led to the construction of the Conflict Dynamics Profile assessment instrument:

Perspective Taking
Creating Solutions
Expressing Emotions
Reaching Out
Reflective Thinking

Delay Responding

Adapting

We will focus on several of these behaviors that we have found most instrumental for dealing with team conflict. In addition, we'll discuss the skills of listening for understanding and demonstrating empathy as they apply to conflict competent teams.

## Reflective Thinking and Delay Responding

In Chapter Three we discussed the usefulness of cooling down and slowing down when confronting an especially disconcerting conflict. There's no doubt that the ability to identify one's rising conflict temperature is critical for ultimately controlling one's emotions. And the concept of slowing things down during conflict makes it easier to believe that the conflict can be addressed effectively. Reflective thinking and delay responding are behaviors that can accomplish the cooling and slowing.

These two skills are closely related but not identical. They share the common characteristics of taking a time-out from the conflict and moving away from the conflict temporarily. During reflective thinking, the team member spends time away from the conflict specifically focusing on what has happened, the impact of the conflict on the parties, and how best to reengage in the discussion. During delay responding, the team member purposely disengages temporarily as completely as possible from the conflict. This distancing from the tension enables the individual to begin cooling down. Use of these behaviors also helps refocus on the task versus relationship conflict. We believe it is less important to distinguish between these two skills than it is to engage in them when handling team conflicts. Therefore, we are addressing both behaviors together.

We have followed the careers of James and Renee for a number of years. Readers of our first book may recall their rather intense conflict during the time when they were leaders of two sales teams in a large pharmaceutical company. James's team seemed to win all the monthly sales awards, and Renee's team typically finished a close second. Bragging rights and award dinners aside, the relationship between James and Renee deteriorated to levels of pettiness and revenge. During one incident, James steadfastly refused to allow Renee to use a large conference room he had reserved, even though his plans had changed and he didn't really need the large space. He later admitted he just wanted to "make her life difficult" at the time. In another instance, Renee pointed out mistakes in James's sales report while James was presenting the report to the executive staff. Renee later acknowledged that the mistakes were very minor but that it was "an opportunity to make him look bad and pay the big creep back." Finally, their boss, Patricia, became involved. She insisted on civility between the two and met with them individually and together. Over time, and with much effort by all parties, it seemed that James and Renee patched up their differences and led their teams to continued success.

Now, several years later, James and Renee have advanced to director-level positions in the organization. In addition to their individual responsibilities, they serve together on a senior team created by the division president, charged with exploring new business development opportunities. Both James and Renee are held in high regard by the organization and are considered high potentials for continued advancement.

During a recent meeting, Renee was delivering a report on the development of a new drug for treating neurological disorders. The preliminary results looked quite promising. Her presentation accurately suggested that this new drug, though still years away from approval, had the potential to lead to unprecedented growth for the company. The entire team was understandably taken by the presentation—the entire team, that is, except for James.

Much of Renee's data had been supplied by a group working in James's business unit. As James listened to her report, he waited patiently for Renee to give credit to his people. He knew the information at least as well as she did, if not better. But that wasn't the issue. "When," he thought, "is she going to acknowledge the work my group put into the research and development of her report? She's making it sound like this is all her doing!"

As James's patience began to grow thin, he found himself feeling frustrated and angry with Renee. He even caught himself thinking about some of the conflicts they had experienced years ago. "Haven't we put all this behind us?" he wondered. As the thought crossed his mind to interrupt her, he decided instead to excuse himself from the meeting. He quietly, and as unobtrusively as possible, exited the meeting room and walked toward the men's room. Once inside, he took a deep breath, looked at himself in the mirror, and began considering what had just transpired.

Despite his best efforts to mask his frustration and slip out of the meeting unnoticed, several team members observed his exit. Tony, one of his best friends, was sitting next to James. Even before James began to push his chair back from the table, Tony knew something was bothering him. As Renee reviewed the prospects of the new drug, Tony saw James shaking his head and tapping his fingers uncharacteristically on his notepad. Just as he was about to ask James if he was all right, James glanced around the room, took a deep breath, and began making his way to the door. Tony wasn't sure, but he had a pretty good idea that James was unhappy with something Renee had said. "Just like old times," he thought. "I wonder what those two are feuding about now?"

Across the room, Yolanda was listening intently to Renee when she caught some movement out of the corner of her eye. She glanced toward the back of the room and watched as James made a beeline for the door. "That's odd," she thought. "Renee is praising the work James's group has completed and he's checking himself out of the meeting. I wonder what he's thinking?"

Nick, seated next to where Renee was standing, also noticed James leaving. As the team leader, Nick was constantly working on keeping his senior-level colleagues focused and energized. Each of them had plenty of responsibilities outside the scope of the team. All Nick ever asked was that the members come to meetings prepared to discuss the topics on the agenda and to be fully engaged during the team meetings. "Bad form, James!" was his conclusion as James closed the door and headed down the hallway. "That's not the level of focus I want from my teammates. I'll have to have a chat with him about this."

Meanwhile, back in the men's room, James began mulling over the situation. First, he took stock of emotions. "I am angry, I am frustrated, and I am surprised. That's interesting," he thought. "Anger and frustration make all kinds of sense. But why am I surprised?" This reflection is critical to James's ability to cool down and slow down. It shows that he is not only identifying his emotions, but he's beginning to wonder why he has them. Awareness enables him to separate himself from the emotion, thus cooling things down. Reflecting enables him to think about his emotions and actions, thus slowing things down.

Next, he considered what he should do about his reaction. At the same time, though, he realized that he needed to get back to the meeting quickly. This was an important session, and he didn't want to miss information or become conspicuous by his absence. Little did he know that he had already had an impact on several team members. Let's consider all of his actions and decisions over the recent minutes to fully appreciate their impact.

When James first experienced his displeasure with Renee's presentation, his senses were heightened. Without knowing for sure, he interpreted or assumed that Renee was not giving credit to his people and that she was doing so purposefully. In other words, he invented Renee's intentions. Very quickly, virtually without thinking, James attributed malevolent motives to Renee, which fed his growing anger, frustration, and surprise. This kind of reaction is almost impossible to control for most of us. When we experience emotions, our brains are flooded with them and essentially unable to replace emotive thinking with rational thinking. And all this is taking place in fractions of seconds. To expect James to make mindful decisions at this instant is nearly impossible. Therefore, we won't dwell on the emergence of James's feelings.

As the seconds passed, James became more aware of his feelings and the words Renee was speaking. With the growing awareness of his anger and frustration, James recalled the advice of his former boss, Patricia. "When you realize that you are having strong feelings about a person or a situation," she counseled, "decide what to do instead of allowing your instincts to decide for you." In this case, he decided to take a walk instead of interrupting Renee's presentation. His decision to delay his response was the first step toward constructively addressing the situation. Imagine the possible consequences had he interrupted. Renee would have been surprised and may have responded poorly. Other team members would have wondered about James's intentions. All of the participants in the meeting would have interpreted an interruption through their own filters, making assumptions and attributions of their own. Certainly some of the members of the team had already been affected just by James's exit from the room, and they would have to deal with their observations and reactions. However, by taking a time-out and choosing not to interrupt, James avoided a potential escalation of the situation and bought himself time to identify, assess, and control his emotions.

While we enthusiastically applaud James's decision to take a time-out and begin reflecting on the situation, it's clear that conflict in a team very quickly touches more than just the two principals. In this case, James put his reflection on hold and rapidly decided to return to the meeting. The longer he was absent, he reasoned, the more likely his teammates might misunderstand. He decided on a course of action that included sending some signals to quell any misperceptions and apologizing to anyone who might have been upset that he left. On his way back down the hallway to the meeting room, he also committed to himself to spend a little time after the meeting revisiting his emotional reaction to Renee's presentation. After all, he only assumed her intent. He didn't actually know what she intended. Once he had a better idea of why he reacted so sharply, he thought he would be in a better position to speak with her about his thoughts and feelings.

When James reentered the meeting room, only a couple of minutes had passed. In that short time span, though, much had occurred. When Renee saw James leaving, she was worried that she might have misrepresented some of his group's findings. Tony assumed that James and Renee were headed for a reprise of conflicts from the old days. Yolanda simply thought it was odd timing and maybe a little rude for James to excuse himself. Nick reasoned that James was just not interested in the presentation and was violating a team agreement about staying focused. As James stepped back into the room, he made eye contact with Renee, smiled, and gave a little wave of his hand, nodded at Nick as he made his way back to his chair, and gave Tony a quick pat on the shoulder as he sat down. When he looked around the room, he momentarily locked eyes with Yolanda who had a quizzical look on her face. He gave her a quick thumbs-up sign and returned his focus to Renee, who was still speaking.

We can tell you that James and Renee spoke about this incident the following day. James, after reflecting on his initial emotions, was able to share his reaction with Renee in a constructive manner. She appreciated his honesty and assured him that she was very appreciative of his group's work. She felt bad that he even fleetingly thought otherwise. In fact, Renee thought that she had made it clear in her remarks that his team had been instrumental in the research. Obviously James heard it differently. In addition, James came to understand his reaction of surprise during Renee's presentation. As they reconciled and healed from conflicts earlier in their careers, James had developed a new-found respect for Renee. That she apparently was not going to acknowledge his team's efforts seemed out of character; it was not her nature. In the old days, he surmised that he probably would not have been surprised at her oversight. Because their relationship had strengthened so much over the years, his misperception of her intent caught him completely by surprise. In this case, the power of reflective thinking enabled James to reconcile his emotions and thoughts with the reality of the situation.

The complexity of handling conflict on teams is sobering. Virtually every action taken by one team member can be interpreted in a variety of ways by different teammates. James demonstrated great restraint by choosing not to interrupt Renee. His decision to take a time-out was exactly the right call. Nevertheless, others around the table noticed and judged his behavior. In addition to giving himself a much needed break, he also sent a variety of unintended signals to his teammates. His brief retreat to the men's room enabled him not only to cool down but to assess the entire situation, including task and relationship conflict. He was able to address any misperceptions of his exit when he returned while still buying more time to reflect on his initial reactions. James handled this episode with aplomb by recognizing the potential impact of his behavior on all of his teammates.

The notions of delaying one's response and reflecting on the available options are easy to understand, but often very challenging to implement. Taking a time-out enables you to slow things down so you can consider what's happening. One excellent suggestion comes from William Ury in his latest book, *The Power of a Positive No* (2007). Ury suggests visualizing how the conflict situation looks from a perspective other than one's own. His metaphor involves "going to the balcony." A person who reflects on the situation as if viewing a play from a balcony is able to see it from a place of safety and as a more objective third party. A brief delay and reflection, James discovered, prevented him from reacting in haste and helped him respond with thoughtfulness.

## Listening for Understanding

A friend of ours, Rick Bommelje, coauthor of *The Listening Leader,* gives participants in his seminars a life-size plastic replica of a human ear to remind them of the value of listening

(Steil and Bommelje, 2004). Stephen Covey, author of *The Seven Habits of Highly Effective People* (1989), suggests that we should "seek first to understand, then to be understood" (p. 235). An axiom passed on in families around the world points out that "we have two ears, one mouth, and they should be used in that proportion." Countless books have been penned, articles written, songs sung, and advice given that underscore the wisdom of effectively listening for understanding. You would think that by now, we would have embraced the message and made listening *the* priority in all of our communications. Apparently not. Sure, we get it on an intellectual level. We comprehend the value of listening for understanding. For many of us, though, turning something that's so obvious cognitively into consistent behavioral practice proves to be surprisingly challenging.

One of our favorite television sitcoms was *Frasier*. The show, starring Kelsey Grammer as a self-absorbed psychologist, made it wonderfully clear that not even a successful psychologist was immune from the perils of poor listening skills, misunderstandings, assumptions, and attributions. Frasier's endless ability to misread, misinterpret, and misjudge situations provided comic relief for millions of viewers over the years. The crowning glory of each show was the moment when Frasier, while hosting his daily radio talk show, would lean into the microphone and declare, "This is Dr. Frasier Crane. I'm listening." Invariably, to our delight, as the caller would begin to describe a personal problem, Frasier would prove himself to be anything but an effective listener.

Like Frasier, many of us consider ourselves good listeners. We know what good listening looks like, and we do our best to practice all the associated nonverbals. First, when listening in person, we make certain to have steady but nonthreatening eye contact. Next, we position our bodies in such a way as to communicate openness to our communication partner. This entails turning toward the speaker, perhaps leaning in ever so slightly to communicate interest and focus, and tilting our head just so to indicate our intent to hear every word. And we never, ever fold our arms across our chest, thereby signaling that we're closed to any new thoughts or ideas. There is nothing wrong with any of these tactics. In fact, practicing effective body posture and eye contact makes sense. But listening, truly listening for understanding, involves much more. And yet some of the best advice for enhancing one's effectiveness often involves more art than science, more subtlety than clarity.

When listening for understanding, it's imperative that you listen with the intent to understand rather than with the intent to respond. (You may want to read that sentence again because it gets to the essence of conflict competence.) This subtle difference in your intent may be indiscernible to the speaker in the moment but profoundly obvious when the listener becomes the speaker. When you are listening to understand, your mind-set is to hear the speaker's meaning. When you are listening to respond, your mind-set is to communicate back to the speaker.

When listening to understand, you are focused solely on grasping the entire message that the speaker is sending. Your purpose is to comprehend the words, understand the context, and appreciate the emotion of the speaker. You are not yet interested in or contemplating what you're going to say in response. Responding, although incredibly important, comes a bit later. For now, the only thing you want to communicate to the speaker is your complete desire to get what he or she is saying.

We suggest approaching your listening with a sense of curiosity and wonder. Think about that. When you are curious about something, you want to know its meaning. Your focus is on understanding whatever it is that you don't quite yet completely comprehend. When was the last time you found yourself genuinely curious about something somebody said or something you encountered? How did it feel? What were you thinking? Didn't you want to learn more?

We recently received an e-mail forwarded by some friends with an amazing magic trick attached. A group of five playing cards was presented on the screen. The instructions said to pick one card among the five, remember it, and then scroll down to the image of five more playing cards. The magician author of the e-mail guaranteed that he would "read our minds" and remove the card we mentally selected from the next grouping of five cards. To our amazement, the trick worked every time. "How in the world was this possible? How did they do that? Wow, this is mind-boggling," we exclaimed to one another. We tried the trick over and over. We increased our speed. We repeated the same card many times in a row ("That'll show the magician!" we thought). Each of us even picked two different cards at the same time. Every time the trick worked. We were blown away. And we wondered how it was done. Heck, we were dying to know how it was done! That's what we mean by curiosity. Go into your conversations with a sense of wonder about what it is you're about to hear. Bring some anticipation that you may hear something new, something novel, or something amazing. When you do, you'll find yourself listening for understanding.

By the way, for those of you who have seen this amazing card trick and don't know how they did that, we've revealed the secret at the end of the Epilogue. It's your choice as to whether you want to see it. Are you curious?

Let's compare the notion of listening for understanding with what happens when we are listening to respond. Listening to respond is tantamount to biding time until it's your turn to speak. We suspect that quite a few people are considered decent communicators even though they practice listening to respond rather than listening for understanding. They may even be held in high regard for their abilities to articulate thoughts clearly, persuade others, give others a chance to speak their minds, and refrain from interrupting. Ironically this type of listener may quite often be reinforced for having good listening skills. They demonstrate the right nonverbal behaviors, so they look as if they're listening. They don't interrupt the speaker, so they appear polite and interested. And when it is "their turn" to speak, they acknowledge points made by others, thereby demonstrating just how much they heard. It sure looks and sounds like good listening. Unfortunately, because this listener's priority is responding, the potential is great that the listener missed the full meaning intended by the speaker. What gets lost for the speaker is the sense of feeling understood by the listener, and what gets lost for the listener is true understanding of the speaker. When this occurs, and we believe it occurs all the time, the potential for misunderstandings and disagreements rises, therefore leading to an increased likelihood for conflict.

In the context of teams, listening to respond rather than listening for understanding can literally lead to misunderstandings about misunderstandings. Imagine if several team members are listening only to respond during a discussion. Before long, no speaker is feeling understood. In well-intended efforts to become understood, voices begin to increase in volume, gestures and tones become more emphatic, and phrases such as, "I hear you, but think about this . . .," become the norm. In their zeal to clarify the nature of the task conflict being discussed, team members unwittingly transform task conflict into relationship conflict. Sound familiar? We have seen team after team fall into this trap.

How easy is it to slip into a difficult situation based solely on a failure to listen for understanding? Consider the following conversation that took place during a team picnic, of all places. The team had been researching client reactions to a potential new product, and the teammates were discussing an upcoming milestone review meeting:

Dave: I'll be sure to bring the results from the client focus group meeting we have scheduled for next Monday.

Jay: That's good, Dave. We'll need those results so we can compare them to the results from the previous focus groups.

Cindy (with eyebrows raised): Aren't the results from the earlier groups old news? Those took place months ago, before we included the new product's specs.

Dave: No problem. The meeting next week will include all the new specs. It wouldn't make sense to use the old model with this group.

Chris: Yeah, but unless we compare the results from before with the current group's response, what's the purpose for having our meeting?

Jay (nodding in agreement): That's my point exactly. We have to compare the responses between and among the various groups.

Cindy (shaking her head): Okay, gang, listen. It doesn't matter anymore what the previous focus groups thought. They were considering an old prototype, not the new one. What's so hard to understand about that?

Dave: I'm not talking about the old prototype. The meeting next week is focused only on the new one. So I'll have client reactions only to the new model.

Jay: Wait! How are we going to do any analysis?

Cindy (speaking before Jay is finished): The focus has to be on the new model.

Chris (holding up her hand): That's true, but we have to consider all the results we gathered from the previous sessions. That's a lot of data.

Jay: I hear that!

Cindy: I don't think you do!

Dave (leaving the table): I need another hot dog.

All four team members in this conversation intended to speak clearly and to be understood. All four tried to emphasize their points and positions. All four heard what the others said, but they did little in attempting to understand. Rather, they resorted quickly to emphasizing their personal points of view. They listened just enough to enable themselves a chance to respond. The result was nothing more than a standoff with no mutual understanding.

Teams that consistently practice listening for understanding position themselves to get the best out of their differences, misunderstandings, and disagreements. They engage conflicting views and interests with the intent to grasp their teammates' ideas rather than argue with them. Conflicts literally become the fertile ground for planting a variety of perceptions that, once understood, can be nurtured into a new crop of ideas and solutions. Listening for understanding is one important skill that enables teams to get the good out of conflict while avoiding the bad.

The differences between listening to respond and listening for understanding may be subtle. The differences in the quality of communications, however, may be profound. And the likelihood that team members find themselves grappling with relationship conflict rather than debating task conflict increases tremendously.

## Perspective Taking and Empathy

We recommend the use of perspective taking and empathy more frequently than any other skills and behaviors for addressing team conflict. The practice of perspective taking includes the ability to see the conflict from another person's point of view. The primary goal is to understand the content of the conflict as completely as possible through conflict partners' eyes. In other words, perspective taking focuses on the task. Empathy is a form of perspective taking focused on emotion rather than content. When you use empathy, your goal is to accurately understand and describe how your conflict partners feel about the situation or issue. Empathy focuses on the relationship. Perspective taking and empathy together form a powerful skill set for demonstrating appreciation of and understanding about the views, interests, feelings, and positions of teammates with whom you are experiencing conflict.

Using perspective taking and demonstrating empathy are closely linked to listening for understanding. In fact, listening for understanding is essentially a prerequisite for effectiveness with these skills. Without understanding, attempts at perspective taking and empathy can fall flat.

One of our clients, a well-known and highly successful invest-ment firm, identifies a group of high-potential leaders each year. The firm has created an eighteen-month developmental experi-ence with both individual opportunities and team projects. One component of the plan is a two-day team retreat at our cam-pus designed to help the team appreciate the differences among them and leverage those differences when addressing business challenges.

An experiential exercise we use with the team to illustrate the power of perspective taking is about a fictitious nuclear waste spill. The team is divided into two squads. One squad is made up of "supervisors" whose job is to survey the site of the spill, create a plan for removing the waste, and provide direction and support for the cleanup. The other squad is the "cleanup crew" made up of "technicians" who will physically conduct the cleanup. The technicians are blindfolded. For the purposes of the storyline, they are wearing "protective eyewear." As you might imagine, there are many rules and regulations regarding the cleanup effort. Safety hazards are abundant and severe. (We won't disclose all the nuances of the exercise here. We want to protect the integrity of the activity so we can use it with you or your team in the future!) Here are a few of the rules and expectations:

- No one can enter the "contamination zone" (a roped-off circle approximately twenty feet in diameter).
- Supervisors cannot touch or use a specialized "tool"; only technicians can use it.
- The "containment unit" (an upside-down five-gallon bucket) may never be touched by anyone, but it must be moved to a safety zone some forty feet away.
- The nuclear waste, "sleazium," may not be spilled (the sleazium is a small ball sitting on top of the inverted bucket),
- Supervisors can provide all the verbal direction they deem appropriate.

- Technicians can communicate fully with the supervisors and each other but may never remove their "protective eyewear."

As the rules and expectations are explained to the supervisors, the complexity of the situation becomes clear. The supervisors must devise a plan for the technicians to implement that will result in transportation of the nuclear waste from a contamination zone to a safety zone. Violations of work rules and safety regulations will result in penalties that may make the task impossible to complete. To make matters worse, the specialized tool appears to be nothing more than a pile of rope, but the supervisors are prohibited from examining it. And, of course, there is a time limit for completion of the task.

In the dialogue that follows, we have noted the identity of each participant with a "T" for technician or "S" for supervisor. See if you can spot attempts at perspective taking and empathy, especially from supervisors, that may not have been as useful as intended. Look also for opportunities where perspective taking or empathy may have been useful.

Midway through the exercise, Bob had become the main voice for the supervisors. Success in this exercise depends on the accurate placement of technicians around the site of the spill. Moving blindfolded technicians to exact locations is no easy task. The communication sounded something like this:

S Bob: Okay, Connie. Move Greg about two steps to the right.

S Connie: Your right or my right?

S Bob (pointing): That way, that way!

T Greg: Which way?

S Connie (guiding Greg by the shoulders): It's fine. Just move over here. You can trust me.

T Greg: This is hard. I can't see anything, you know.

S Connie: I know. You're in good hands.

S Bob: Rick, you've got to position your guy closer to the circle.

S Rick: Which guy? I'm kind of working with Keith and Mark at the same time.

S Bob: Keith. I mean Mark. Geez!

T Keith: So what do you want me to do?

S Rick: No, not you Keith. I'm moving Mark.

T Keith: So you don't want me to move?

S Evelyn (shouting): Keith, stop moving! Somebody get over there!

S Bob: Keith, I'm coming. You can't move unless one of us is with you.

T Mark: Is that you, Rick?

S Rick: Yeah, I'm with you buddy. Let's just move a few steps toward the tree.

T Mark: Tree? What tree?

S Rick: Sorry, man. (Rick tugs on Mark's arm.) It's over this way.

T Mark: I have no sense of direction or where we are.

S Rick: It doesn't matter right now. I've got you. Time is running out.

T Keith: Can the supervisors agree on one person in charge? Just one voice?

S Evelyn: What should I do with Erica?

S Bob: Erica just needs to stay put. We've got to get Greg farther to the right, I think. Connie, can you move Greg more that direction? (pointing)

T Greg (exasperated): This way, that way! Can't you guys just use "left" and "right"?

S Connie: Hey, everyone, we have to tell our technicians "left" and "right"!

T Greg: Thank you.

S Connie: Make sure to listen. We've got to get this right.

T Greg: You want me to move to the right?

S Connie: No! Correct. Wait! I meant to say "correct," not "right." (laughing) Arrgh, this is driving me crazy!

T Vanessa (standing blindfolded alone): Hello. Nobody's
    talking to me. Do I need to do anything?

S Rick: No, you're fine.

S Bob: All right, now everybody needs to begin lowering their
    rope very slowly.

T Keith: Now?

T Mark: How slowly?

T Erica: How far?

T Vanessa: Me too?

T Greg: Memo to the supervisors: we can't see!

S Bob: We understand that. You've all got to work together
    now. On the count of three, we start lowering. One, two . . .

S Evelyn: Wait, everyone's not lowering!

S Connie: Stop! Stop! We're way off-center.

T Keith: Can just one person talk at a time? This is very
    confusing.

S Bob: Yes. Good idea. Listen to my voice. We can do this.

Amazingly the team was successful in moving the sleazium to
the safety zone. Their triumph of success, the completion of the
task, was dampened, though, as we discussed the effectiveness
of their communication. Although this was just an exercise, some
strain was placed on relationships during the process. Not unlike
many real job-related challenges, failure to effectively perspec-
tive-take and empathize began to take a toll on team members.
Let's first review how the technicians summarized their experiences after the exercise.

Greg described his experience as frustrating and difficult:
"It was very frustrating for me. Being blindfolded, I was reliant
on others, and that's not my style. No one seemed to understand that having my sight removed was not just a handicap for
completing the task; it was disconcerting. Connie was reassuring. That was nice. But I don't think she really understood how
uncomfortable I was." Greg, like most other people, wanted to get
the job done successfully. He was looking for good directions.

But he wanted something more. His biggest frustration was that no one understood how he was feeling. He wanted and needed a small dose of empathy. Recall the strong language he used with words like *disconcerting* and *uncomfortable*. The absence of empathy in Greg's case resulted in frustration.

Keith's experience was similar to Greg's but focused more on the nature of the team's communication. "I'm glad we succeeded," he said. "But honestly, I'm surprised. It was so confusing to have more than one supervisor giving directions. I tried to ask questions but sometimes felt like my questions were annoying the others. I just wanted to know what to do." For Keith, the number of perspectives being given at any one time was confusing. His focus was on the task. He needed others to provide perspective so he could have a mental image of the situation. But he needed the perspectives, the directions, to be presented in an orderly fashion. His pleas for "one voice" seemed to fall on deaf ears.

Mark described the exercise as fun and interesting. He admitted to not knowing where he was and having no sense of direction, but he also said that he is very comfortable in new situations, and he's comfortable without much structure. Mark summarized his experience this way: "I had a good time. I thought it was funny how the supervisors forgot that we couldn't see and referred to trees or told us to move this way or that way. I wouldn't say we had the most effective communication. The exercise very nicely illustrated the need for checking for understanding." Mark had no negative feelings or perceptions with the exercise. His point about checking for understanding, though, underscores the importance of perspective taking as a tool for ensuring the team stays on track. The supervisors were surprised to hear Mark describe the experience as fun. They assumed that all the technicians would find being blindfolded somewhat troubling. This is a case where putting oneself in another's shoes wasn't enough for accurate understanding. Perspective taking and empathy require checking and asking questions to verify well-intended assumptions about the perceptions of others.

Erica said very little during the exercise, and her comments afterward illustrated why: "I just didn't know what to do. I was afraid to move or pull on my rope because I never had a good mental picture of what we were doing. I was happy to do what I was told, but would have felt a lot better if I had the big picture in my head." Erica provides a good example of how it's easy to forget our quieter teammates and assume that silence equals understanding or agreement. Active empathizing and perspective taking with Erica may have uncovered her concerns and helped her participate more effectively.

Vanessa was left "unsupervised" for much of the activity. There were four supervisors and five technicians. Each supervisor paired up with one technician, which left a single technician, Vanessa, alone. Fortunately, Vanessa, much like Mark, was pretty comfortable with the exercise. Being blindfolded posed no serious discomfort for her. However, she was dismayed at being left alone for so much of the activity. "I just wondered why nobody seemed to be talking to me for much of the time. I could hear other technicians receiving directions from a supervisor, but I didn't get much attention unless I asked. Even then, the supervisors just sort of shouted to me about what to do. I actually was a bit lonely." The supervisors were understandably focused on the challenging task at hand. The danger of such intense focus led to Vanessa's feeling a bit forgotten or isolated. An acknowledgment of her feelings would have gone a long way toward reassuring her of her importance to the team effort.

As a group, the supervisors, Bob, Connie, Evelyn, and Rick, were pleased to have successfully completed the task. As they listened to the comments of the technicians, they reflected on their intentions, actions, and assumptions. They admitted to focusing much more on the challenge of moving the sleazium safely than on the perceptions and feelings of the technicians. Bob said, "It never occurred to me that a blindfolded technician could have a good idea about how to move the bucket. I mean, they couldn't see. I wish I would have listened a little more to their ideas. I think Keith and Greg actually had it figured out before we did, but we weren't interested in their blindfolded views!" The lesson here is that everyone has a perspective. Active perspective taking helps uncover hidden or unseen information and viewpoints.

Connie was dismayed at her lack of empathy, especially toward Greg and Vanessa. She was shocked at recalling what she said to Greg: "Make sure to listen. We've got to get this right." Not only did she further confuse him, she was concerned only about the task. She normally prides herself on being empathetic and reassuring. She remembered seeing Vanessa standing alone several times but didn't think to go to her because she was so focused on helping Greg.

Rick hung his head in mock shame and laughed at himself as he remembered one of his responses to Mark. Mark had just described how he had no sense of direction at all. Rick replied in part, "It doesn't matter." Shaking his head in disbelief, Rick pondered aloud, "How could it not matter? I can't believe how little I cared about what Mark was experiencing."

Evelyn decided in advance that she would hang back and let other supervisors take the lead. As a result, she thought she had contributed to the team's effort by not adding to the confusion of several supervisors talking at once. Upon reflection, she proffered a different assessment: "I wish I had attended more to the technicians. It's obvious now that we literally left them in the dark. By not engaging them as partners, we made lots of assumptions about what they were thinking and feeling. As a consequence, we didn't take advantage of their ideas or provide all the support they needed. I can see how easy it is to turn a problem into a conflict."

Teams that use perspective taking skillfully and demonstrate empathy for one another are positioned for addressing conflicts with confidence. When conflicts arise, team members are able to demonstrate respect for and understanding of others' points of view. And beyond that, they may find that their own views substantially expand when focused on understanding others' perspectives. The debate necessary to fully embrace task conflict is enriched. As individual views expand, so does the field of opportunity for the team. The team is able to capitalize on differing views rather than be blocked by them. Similarly, as teammates demonstrate empathy, the emotional connections among teammates are bolstered, and the likelihood for spiraling into the grasp of relationship conflict is diminished. Showing respect for differing views is often easier in a business context than showing regard for others' feelings. When teammates demonstrate genuine regard for each others' feelings, everyone feels validated and safe. When teammates feel safe, they are more likely to share different or opposing views. And perhaps most important, as individual views expand, so does the field of opportunity for the team.

The impact of perspective taking and empathy goes well beyond handling conflict. The impact can be huge in terms of task completion, goal accomplishment, and achievement in general. The challenging issues that most teams face can be met and overcome when everyone's views are considered and understood. Perspective taking is a powerful way to discover, understand, and use the diversity of thoughts and ideas on a team. The impact of empathy is no less critical. The creation and maintenance of relationships among team members is crucial for supporting the team climate. Teams whose members acknowledge others' feelings and demonstrate understanding of others' emotions are much more likely to develop a high degree of trust. When team members show genuine empathy and demonstrate real understanding by accurately describing the feelings of their teammates, the team climate is enriched beyond words.

## Expressing Emotions

Somewhere between an angry outburst and silent simmering lies the elegant middle ground of expressing emotions effectively. In between a sarcastic comment and acquiescence is a place where honest descriptions of feelings live. When team members are skilled at expressing their emotions mindfully, the discussions of conflicting ideas, issues, interests, and positions can become robust without causing damage. The problem is that when dealing with difficult issues, many of us hide our true feelings from our teammates, sometimes resulting in unexpected surges of emotion that are difficult to control. When this occurs, we may lash out, shut down, demean others, or otherwise say or do things that we later regret. Such behavior can lead to the emotional demoralization of the entire team or incite other team members to respond in kind. At either extreme, the results are horrible. A far better alternative is for team members to develop their skills of effectively expressing emotions in a team context.

First, let's consider the case of a team member who hides his emotions. Jerry is director of a large conference center in the Midwest that hosts meetings, corporate retreats, and training seminars and provides the full range of lodging, food service, and meeting support services. The center wants to hire a new manager of conference services. Jerry created a selection team to conduct interviews of several top candidates referred by the organization's employment specialist. On the team are:

- Becky, the manager of food services
- Sue, the manager of lodging
- Mike, the manager of audiovisual support
- Murray, the manager of human resources

The team has completed interviews with the three top candidates and is meeting to make a hiring decision. The meeting has been in progress for approximately an hour:

Jerry: So where does that leave us?
Sue: It looks to me like we're in agreement that of the three candidates, Luke is definitely the weakest. I suggest we decide between Brice and Taylor.

Mike: I agree. I'm ready to eliminate Luke from consideration.

Murray: Me too. Becky?

Becky: I guess I can go along with that. I'm a little concerned that we're selling Luke short on his organizational skills. But of the three, I agree that he's the weakest. What do you think, boss?

Jerry: I'm comfortable if all of you are comfortable.

Mike: You spoke pretty highly of Luke earlier, Jerry. Are you sure?

Jerry: I'm fine with the team's call on this.

Sue: Well then, let's move on. (pointing to the whiteboard) We've already listed the comparative strengths and weaknesses of each candidate. Why don't we each make a case for our personal top choice—either Taylor or Brice?

Murray: Sounds good. Shall we go for it?

(Becky and Mike nod in agreement.)

Jerry: Who's first?

(Sue, Murray, Mike, and Becky each declare their top choice and summarize their rationale. Taylor and Brice each have two votes.)

Becky: Well Jerry, it looks like it's up to you. It's two to two in the bottom of the ninth!

Jerry: Thanks, but the whole reason we put together a team was to make a group decision. It shouldn't come down to me.

Mike: But you're part of the team. Just because you're the last one to speak doesn't really mean it's up to you. What if you had voted earlier?

Jerry (looking down at his notes): True. I just don't have a strong opinion.

Sue: Well, what do you think of our opinions?

Jerry: You all make good points.

Sue: So you're happy with the fact that the four of us disagree?

Jerry: Why wouldn't I be?

Murray (sighing): So how do you want to break the tie?

Jerry: I'm not sure.

Becky: Jerry, I'm going to go out a limb here. I don't think you were happy when we eliminated Luke. Is that right?

(Jerry tilts his head slightly and raises an eyebrow but doesn't say anything.)

Becky: I noticed that you haven't said anything or asked any questions while we've debated Taylor and Brice.

Mike: Are you upset that we dropped Luke?

Sue: Do you think that was a bad call?

Jerry: It doesn't matter. It was a team decision.

Murray: Of course, it matters. We all want to make the best decision. If you're holding back, it's not fair to the team. You may have thoughts or feelings that we haven't considered.

Jerry: I think the best course of action is to abide by the decisions we've already made. My feelings aren't hurt.

Sue: So you didn't want to eliminate Luke.

Jerry (beginning to sound irritated): Look, can we just forget Luke? We need to decide between the remaining two.

Mike: Maybe we should take a quick break first. I know I could use one.

Jerry: Fine. Let's come back in ten minutes.

The team members silently left the conference room. Mike and Sue ducked into Sue's office while Becky and Murray walked to the break room. As soon as he shut the door to Sue's office, Mike said, "Do you believe him? Why is he so afraid to admit that he's upset with our decision?" At almost the same moment, Becky was pouring a cup of coffee and said to Murray, "What is up with Jerry? If he's surprised at our thoughts about Luke, why doesn't he just say so?" Meanwhile, Jerry walks toward his office. As he passes by Darcy, his assistant, he remarks just loud enough for her to hear, "I don't know why I trusted them with this decision in the first place."

Why is Jerry suppressing his feelings, even when directly asked by others? Many people believe that sharing their feelings is either a sign of weakness or that by sharing, they will hurt somebody else's feelings. Some refuse to share when they are in disagreement with others as an ill-informed signal of their displeasure. Still others may not share if they feel unsafe or at risk by their disagreement.

What is the cost of Jerry's suppressing his feelings? First, he's not being honest with his teammates. As they begin to sense that he's concealing or holding back, the fragile fabric of trust begins to erode. Second, keeping his displeasure or concern bottled up leads to an increase in his emotional blood pressure. In other words, what were once mild feelings of concern or surprise grow into more intense feelings as he broods and simmers. Next, team members grow exasperated with Jerry's steadfast deflections of their questions and genuine interest in his thoughts and feelings. Finally, all parties begin to attribute negative or suspicious intent to others. In this case, not only is the decision-making task gridlocked, the relationships among team members are strained.

Next, let's consider the consequences of the other extreme. What happens when team members express emotions poorly by displaying anger or demeaning others? Imagine how the meeting might have proceeded if Jerry were the type to express his feelings without regard for others. Instead of attempting to keep his true feelings under wraps, what if Jerry had reacted to the proposal to eliminate Luke differently?

Jerry: So where does that leave us?

Sue: It looks to me like we're in agreement that of the three candidates, Luke is definitely the weakest. I suggest we decide between Brice and Taylor.

Mike: I agree. I'm ready to eliminate Luke from consideration.

Murray: Me too. Becky?

Becky: I guess I can go along with that. I'm a little concerned that we're selling Luke short on his organizational skills. But of the three, I agree that he's the weakest. What do you think boss?

Jerry: Are you out of your minds? (his voice rises) Eliminate Luke at this point? What isn't there to like about him? I don't get it!

(Silent stares emanate from the other team members. Finally Murray speaks.)

Murray: Uh, Jerry. I guess you think Luke is the best of the three?

Jerry: That's not what I'm saying at all! Don't put words in my mouth. I'm saying this may be the most important decision we make all year. And you guys want to eliminate one of our top three choices already! That doesn't make sense.

Sue (after another awkward pause): All right, so maybe we should consider all three candidates for a while longer. We've got their strengths and weaknesses listed on the whiteboard. Who wants to continue?

(More silence.)

The meeting ended after another ten minutes of fitful and tentative discussion.

Mike finally suggested that they stop, spend time reviewing the candidates, and reconvene again in the morning. As they filed out of the conference room, no one spoke. Jerry headed back to his office, and the others made their way to the break room, where Mike said, "Do you believe him? If he's upset with our decision, why doesn't he just say so instead of blasting us?" Becky, pouring a cup of coffee, offered, "I don't know what's up with him. If he's surprised that we moved too quickly to eliminate Luke, he could just point it out to us." Meanwhile, Jerry walked toward his office. As he passed by Darcy, his assistant, he remarked just loud enough for her to hear, "I don't know why I trusted them with this decision in the first place."

Why might Jerry express such anger and hostility so openly? Some people don't understand the impact of such behavior or may believe that it's best to let people know exactly and emphatically where they stand at all times. In this case, Jerry was upset with the team and decided he needed to let them know.

What is the cost of such overtly aggressive behavior? First, displaying outright anger seldom results in a better discussion. In fact, the exact opposite is true: it exacerbates relationship conflict. Discussion and interaction are squelched, so effective decision making and problem solving are virtually impossible. Second, hostile and accusatory behavior never contributes to a team's climate. As we've discussed before, establishing and maintaining a safe, open environment is critical for the development of team conflict competence. Next, as in the other extreme, team members grew exasperated with Jerry, this time in reaction to his unexpected and unabashed criticism of the team. Finally, also as before, all parties began to attribute negative or suspicious intent to others. Again, the decision-making task was gridlocked and relationships among team members teetered on the brink.

The middle ground of expressing emotions effectively is achieved through a combination of efforts. Team members must first be able to identify and understand their emotions. Then, as the feelings and emotions become apparent to them during interactions with teammates, they will be better positioned to control those emotions. Controlling is the heart of effective expression. The key is a person's ability to describe his or her feelings and the willingness to disclose such descriptions to teammates. In Jerry's case, he could have expressed his emotions effectively early in the discussion in several ways:

"I have a different view of Luke. I actually found a lot to like about him. I'm not comfortable eliminating him yet. Can we continue to discuss him for a while longer?"

"Wow, I'm surprised that I see it so differently. Can I summarize my thoughts about Luke with you?"

"I'm a little concerned. I wonder if it's too early to eliminate anybody yet. This is an important decision. I remember being frustrated at moving too quickly on some hiring decisions in the past. I don't want to miss anything that we might regret later."

The point is to describe your thoughts, views, or feelings in a way that lets others know where you stand without acting out your emotions or concealing them. One way to think about it is empathizing with yourself. Just as we advocate doing your best to label the feelings of others as a way to demonstrate empathy, effectively expressing emotions includes labeling your own feelings and disclosing them to others. This can be difficult or risky, especially if the team climate isn't quite perfect. But expressing emotions effectively is one of myriad behaviors that contribute to the team's climate because it helps take the heat out of conflicts. The more teammates do it, the better the climate is and the easier it is to continue expressing emotions effectively.

Had Jerry effectively expressed his emotions to the team, it's easy to imagine the course the discussion would have taken. Murray, Sue, Mike, and Becky would have appreciated Jerry's candor and willingness to share his feelings and views. It takes a certain amount of courage to admit seeing an issue differently or to disclose an emotion to others. Expressing such thoughts and feelings requires a bit of vulnerability that demonstrates trust in teammates. When teammates practice the effective expression of their emotions, the climate is right for the kind of deep and robust discussions that lead to more informed decision making and novel approaches to issues. The delicate balance between task and relationship conflict is more effectively maintained. Conflicts are easier to address and are seen not only as interesting challenges but as prime opportunities. As the confidence and competence of team members grow, so does the confidence and competence of the team. Teams begin finding ways to harvest the positives from conflict while eradicating the negatives.

## Conclusion

All teams experience conflict at some point. When they do, the conflict can follow one of two paths. When team members get stuck in the rightness of their positions, refuse to engage in discussion, accuse others of heinous motives, and otherwise ineffectively respond, the conflict follows a destructive path. It can almost suck the life out of a team, causing stress, demoralization, hopelessness, and eventual failure of the team to perform. But when team members explore the nature of the conflict, share their differing perspectives, examine the issues, respect one another's emotions, and identify and control their own feelings, conflict travels on a constructive and often very useful path. Team tasks are accomplished, new ideas emerge, and team relationships are valued. They discover that they are getting the best out of task conflict while avoiding the worst aspects of relationship conflict.

The secret to constructive conflict is that there is no secret at all. Team leaders and team members individually and collectively have the power to choose the way they interact and communicate with each other. When they choose wisely, the intensity of conflict remains manageable. Differences and misunderstandings are addressed comfortably. Disagreements are met with curiosity rather than animosity. The ways team members choose to communicate essentially creates the map that conflict will follow. The better able team members are to engage, speak, listen, hear, interpret, and respond constructively, the more likely their teams are to leverage conflict rather than be leveled by it.

## Components for Building Conflict Competent Teams

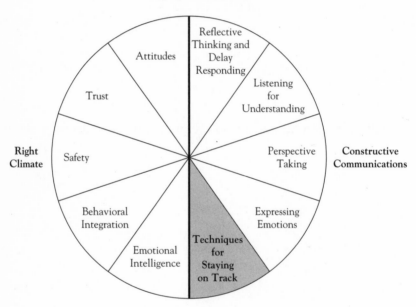

# 5

# TECHNIQUES FOR STAYING ON TRACK

In great teams conflict becomes productive.
The free flow of conflicting ideas is critical for
creative thinking, for discovering new solutions no
one individual would have come up with on his own.
—*Peter Senge*

By now it is clear that conflict on teams is inevitable, so trying to avoid conflict at all costs does not work. The conflict simply goes underground and infects relationships and decision making in sometimes less obvious but equally destructive ways. The tactic of arguing vehemently for one's position may result in temporary "victory," but it handicaps long-term relationships and the ability to resolve future conflicts. Other variations of destructive choices during conflict such as yielding, sarcasm, blocking, and hiding emotions also prove to be just as ineffective.

Making constructive choices, especially in the moment, is not always easy. As we have seen, even when some team members behave effectively, their conflict partners do not always respond in kind. Task conflict morphs into relationship conflict. The resulting heat and emotion that come with such conflict cause even the most level-headed of us to make dubious choices at times. So what's a team to do?

For times when the safety and trust of an effective team climate doesn't translate to quick resolutions or the best intentions for constructive communication seem to fall flat, we suggest a variety of techniques and processes. First, we offer a word of caution about selecting and implementing these techniques.

*There is no substitute for establishing the right climate and choosing constructive communication behaviors.* The tools and techniques we suggest here, especially when used in isolation, cannot be relied on to replace safety, trust, and effective communication. The purpose of these techniques and tools is to assist teams in preparing for conflicts in advance and to address conflicts when they're stuck. These tools and techniques work best for teams that have a solid climate and consistently use constructive communication skills. When conflicts get tough, techniques such as these can help teams identify, assess, control, and overcome obstacles. It's in this spirit that we describe these techniques for building and maintaining conflict competent teams.

We also wish to point out that some of these techniques are best used with the assistance of a facilitator. Teams may decide in some cases that the team leader can play this role. In other cases, it may be better to select a person not affiliated with the team for assistance. In every case, we clearly state our recommendation regarding the use of a facilitator.

We describe a number of techniques and tools as they apply to the life cycle of conflicts. This context enables team members to select techniques for application at the right time. We have identified three time frames that describe the sequence of events in conflicts: before, during, and after. *Before* refers to periods of time where no conflicts are yet apparent. *During* is the most familiar time frame: conflict is clearly present, and team members are having difficulty making progress. *After* is the period of time following a conflict that has been apparently resolved.

## Before

It may seem a bit odd to suggest the use of techniques that will help unlock conflict before it happens. How do team members know they need a technique before conflict? The answer is they don't. What teams must believe, though, is that they will encounter conflict. Even teams with the best climate and the most constructive communications skills will encounter conflict. Understanding this eventuality makes it prudent that teams choose several practices or techniques that can help them prepare for the inevitability of conflict.

## Team Agreements

Many highly effective teams create, publish, and commit to a list of agreements that describe how they will interact with one another as a team. These lists may include team norms, operating principals, rules of interaction, team values, meeting procedures, and other ground rules for ensuring constructive communication among teammates and the maintenance of a safe team environment. Such agreements provide a foundation that secures a team when the going gets tough. Unfortunately, most teams that invite us to assist when they are having conflict have not drawn up team agreements in advance. Often we suggest that they do so as insurance against future conflicts.

There are many processes a team can follow to create team agreements. Sometimes teams find it helpful to seek the assistance of a facilitator who can provide objective observations about their process and suggest a structure for creating the agreements. We suggest eight simple elements or steps to the process:

- *Step 1: Review the team's mission and context.* This step, which doesn't have to take long, provides context for the agreements. Assuming that all team members have the same understanding of the team's mission is dangerous. It is best to clarify, discuss, and agree on what the team is charged to accomplish. It may be valuable to invite the team's sponsor to review the team's mission or goal so there is no misunderstanding.
- *Step 2: Discuss the desired climate.* Team members are encouraged to describe how they would like to work together. It can be beneficial for team members to share stories about previous positive experiences they have had on other teams. All team

members should share their views. In fact, this step should not be taken if all members cannot participate. We sometimes ask team members to independently list words and phrases that describe the nature of interactions they would most like to experience on the team. Then we ask them to share their lists while one person records the terms on a flip chart. Creating a comprehensive description of the desired climate or atmosphere for the team will lead to the productive generation of ideas in the next step.

• *Step 3: Brainstorm suggestions for creating the climate.* Brainstorming techniques vary. What is critical is that all voices are heard, every suggestion is recorded, debate regarding the suggestions is disallowed, and each idea is regarded as valuable. We advise that the ideas generated in this step be in the form of behavioral or process suggestions. For example, it is more useful to suggest, "All team members will ask questions when they don't understand," rather than, "Check for understanding." This nuance will be very useful later in the process.

• *Step 4: Combine similar suggestions.* This is a step in most classic brainstorming processes. When team members are uninhibited during the brainstorming step, many similar ideas naturally appear. Because of the sheer volume of suggestions, combining similar ideas lends to the efficiency of the process while reducing potential misunderstandings.

• *Step 5: Prioritize suggestions.* Referring to the discussion and descriptions of the team's desired climate, team members can begin analyzing the list of suggestions. Again, classic brainstorming techniques can be applied here. What is most critical is that the list of suggestions is pared down to a length complete enough to create and support the desired climate yet concise enough to guide team meetings and interactions without complexity. We usually recommend no fewer than five and no more than ten independent team agreements. We always recommend the creation of some agreements that specifically address the eventuality of conflict.

• *Step 6: Behaviorize the remaining suggestions.* As we suggested in step 3, it is most useful to create agreements that focus on specific behaviors or accepted processes. This characteristic brings life to the agreements. For instance, an agreement stating, "Each team member will show respect to every other teammate by listening without interruption," provides a much clearer and actionable mental picture than, "Respect everyone at all times." The goal is to create agreements that are simple, clear, and suggestive of constructive behavior.

• *Step 7: Record and distribute the list.* Once the list evolves into statements of behavior and process, it should be recorded and distributed to team members for reflection. We suggest establishing a second meeting time to discuss and complete the list. Team members then have time to review and consider each of the suggested agreements without the pressure of quick decisions or commitments. A single overnight break is usually sufficient. The time frame can be shorter or longer if necessary. The key is to provide time for all participants to feel comfortable with their reflection.

• *Step 8: Review and finalize agreements.* The team should set aside a time to review the suggested agreements, entertain modifications, and commit to the final list of team agreements. We suggest that each team member signify his or her commitment verbally once the final list is presented. We also suggest that teams review their list of agreements periodically and provide a mechanism for revising the agreements when circumstances warrant.

The establishment of team agreements is a good practice for all teams. This will not, however, prevent conflicts from arising. In fact, we hope that the establishment of team agreements will result in the acknowledgment of more differences rather than fewer. We hope that it leads to vigorous debates of conflicts and robust exploration of ideas. In short, we hope that the commitment to team agreements provides a foundation for embracing conflict on teams and using it as an advantage for solving complex problems, making tough decisions, and meeting serious challenges.

## Structured Disclosure

The very term *structured disclosure* seems a little confusing. Disclosure, especially at a personal level, seems more genuine if it occurs naturally, without the pressure of process or expectation. We agree. The suggestion of a technique that elicits disclosure in no way replaces good-old-fashioned, spur-of-the-moment, from-the-gut expressions of true feelings or points of view. The technique can, however, result in a significant sharing of experiences that can bolster a team that is facing conflicts or other hardships.

In the early stages of a team's existence, or at least at a time when no conflict is apparent, we suggest that team members take some time to share views, thoughts, unique perspectives, and experiences. Such sharing can result in sometimes surprisingly significant insights. And it helps build trust and camaraderie that provides insulation against the hard reality of inevitable conflicts in the future.

When engaging with a team for the first time, we usually conduct some kind of ice-breaking introductory activity. This practice is generally expected and routine. Never wishing to be perceived as routine, we enjoy finding ways to involve the team members that result in new understanding and appreciation of one another. Lots of introductory activities are fun. We advocate fun. We also advocate methods that include at least a dash of depth and meaning. That's where structured disclosure got its start.

We find that this technique works best with teams that have been in existence for a while. It's a bit more challenging in these cases but can result in intriguing connections and insights. We begin by asking team members to share several routine bits of information about themselves. The list varies, but in addition to their name, we usually ask for their home town, years of experience in the organization, and area of specialty. Then to the list, we add this item: "Plus, tell us something interesting or unique about yourself that nobody else in the room yet knows."

We watch with interest (and a little amusement) as eyebrows rise, teammates glance at each other, heads are scratched, and chins rubbed. Finally, someone will ask, "You mean something that nobody else in the room knows, not even one other person?" "Yes," we reply. "We think you'll find this interesting and maybe even entertaining!"

What results ranges from ordinary to sublime, hilarious to sobering, insightful to amazing. Instantly, as teammates share, new connections are made and respect grows. Teammates look at one another in a slightly different light. Questions one would never think of asking another are now perched on curious lips. "You grew up in Meridian, Mississippi! I lived just down the road in a tiny place called Toomsuba! When did you live there?" one teammate exclaimed to another. "I didn't know you were a musician. I played the clarinet all through high school. Do you still play?" asked another. "Wow, I once met President Clinton too! It was at a town hall meeting. How did you meet him?" The sharing becomes contagious. Learning something new about one another creates interest, intrigue, and trust. The base is strengthened, the foundation fortified. Everyone on the team is just a bit more connected to one another.

Of course, not every revelation is profound, nor does it need to be. The simple act of sharing something previously unrevealed to others is the essence of relationship building. And as relationships on the team are strengthened, so is the team's ability to face conflict constructively when it occurs. Structured disclosure, as a technique before conflict happens, may prove to be a significant hedge against the harmful effects of conflict and an added support for getting the best from it.

## Predicting Hot Topics

How often do the members of teams know that particular topics are going to be too hot to handle? Think about your team or teams. Are there certain topics or issues that are off-limits for the team to discuss? We bet there are.

Some of the groundbreaking work on organizational conflict was conducted by Chris Argyris, who described the development of a team's "collective cooling system" through the constructive discussion of task and relationship issues that otherwise would become "undiscussables" (Argyris, 1990). The trick is to surface such undiscussables in ways that enable rather than stifle hearty conversation and debate.

We once worked with the leadership team at a local middle school: the principal, assistant principal, two guidance counselors, the office manager, and several department heads. The original purpose for our engagement with the team was to provide some team-building exercises to help kick off a new school year. We soon found that the team was facing some serious and potentially debilitating disagreements.

During the team discussion after one of the exercises, two team members engaged in a lively debate about the method the team used to solve the problem. The debate didn't appear particularly problematic to us. We made sure all points of view were heard, summarized the key learnings from the exercise, and suggested a short break before starting another exercise. The assistant principal approached us in the hallway and said, "What you just saw is pretty much par for the course around here. Those two seem to go at it all the time. And if it's not those two, it's somebody else. It seems like conflicts flare up, flame out quickly, then go underground all the time." We decided that rather than move ahead with the next exercise, we would investigate a bit further by engaging the team in more discussion. What we found was almost exactly what the assistant principal had described. The team readily admitted that they had differences of opinion frequently. They also admitted that they seldom discussed conflicts long enough to reach settlements or agreements. When we asked what prevented them from debating issues thoroughly enough to reach conclusions, we were met with mostly blank stares and silence. Finally, one of the guidance counselors suggested, "I think there are some topics that are just taboo for us." A few others nodded in agreement.

Without thinking too deeply and admittedly with some naiveté, we asked, "What topics are those?" This time a few of the team members laughed quietly. Then once again the room fell silent. Finally we said, "Really, we're curious and would like to know. We also think it will be helpful for you to list topics and issues that seem off-limits." Finally, one of the department heads suggested, "The duty list." Another offered, "Student discipline committee." Soon we had a list of almost a dozen topics. Each of the topics was important and necessary for the team to address. What seemed to cause the team's avoidance were not the topics themselves, but the fear that team members would disagree, argue, take sides, and generate bad feelings.

The listing of taboo topics in and of itself did not result in the immediate resolution of the team's conflict. It did unfreeze their collective perception that certain topics were off-limits. Over time, the team found that by addressing each topic independently, they actually made progress. The simple act of identifying their hot topics enabled the team to look at the list objectively, resulting in a sense of more control over how they would address them.

## Describing Desired Outcomes

This technique is an extension of one of the best practices for conducting effective meetings. Our colleague Sharon Grady shared with us an axiom she uses with teams whenever they're about to go into challenging meetings. She notes that how a discussion or topic is set up has a lot to do with how the conversation goes. Steven Covey (1989) suggests beginning with the end in mind. No matter how they frame it, teams that begin discussions or meetings by describing their desired outcomes for the session find it easier to stay focused and assess their progress.

How often have you found yourself wondering if the team meeting you are attending has any purpose at all? When was the last time you found your mind drifting away during a meeting because you didn't understand why a particular discussion was taking place? Have you ever found yourself entangled in a debate that seemed to have nothing to do with the topic? If you answered yes to any of these questions, you are in good company. An effective way to prevent such predicaments is by beginning team meetings with a description of the results and outcomes expected.

The key to using desired outcomes effectively is being clear about how the desired outcomes are stated. We recommend using statements that leave as little as possible to the imagination. For instance, rather than saying, "Discuss compensation rates for trainers," it may be more useful to say, "Agree on a comprehensive compensation structure for senior instructors." Of course, if the true purpose of the meeting is to "discuss" rather than "agree," say so! The purpose of stating desired outcomes is to provide focus and eliminate misunderstandings that can lead to conflict. The next logical step after stating the desired outcomes is the creation of a plan or process for the discussion that gives the team the best chance of achieving those outcomes. The ultimate value of stating desired outcomes is the team's ability to stay on task. Teams that know where they are going and why they are going there encounter fewer problems on the trip.

## Preliminary Perspective Sharing

One of the surest and simplest ways to set the stage for a potentially contentious team meeting is by inviting all members to quickly and concisely state their starting views without interruption or debate by others. The emphasis here is on "quick" and "concise." The outcome of this technique is a shared awareness of the differences and similarities among team members. This technique greatly reduces the impact of assumptions that are invariably brought to meetings by all parties. It also provides a sense of fairness in that all members are heard before discussions begin in earnest.

A great illustration of this technique is provided by a type of exercise we turn to often in our classes. The use of synergy exercises is common for raising awareness and building skill in team problem-solving and decision-making contexts. The concept of synergy is that the sum can be greater than the individual parts. In other words, the solutions or decisions reached by a single person may not be as valuable or thorough as those made through sharing perspectives and combining resources. Several classic synergy survival exercises have been used for years. You may recognize some of them: Jungle Survival, Lifeboat, Stranded on the Moon, Lost in the Desert, and many others. In each exercise, participants are asked to independently rank-order a list of items or place a series of actions in sequence. Then a group or team meets to reach a consensus ranking on the same items or actions. The individual and team answers are then compared to the order created by a group of experts. The idea is that the consensus order will be closer to the experts' suggestions than the average of the individual rankings. When this occurs, synergy is reached.

Over the years, we have observed an interesting phenomenon. At times, we provide different levels of structure for the team consensus discussions. In some cases we simply give the team a specific amount of time during which they must agree on a team answer. In other cases, we suggest that each team member have a short timed period (usually one to two minutes) to review his or her rank order and a bit of rationale for it. Each team member has the floor for that time. No interruptions and no discussion are allowed until each individual has been heard. Then the team is given a time frame during which they must agree on their consensus team rank order. Teams that begin with individual presentations first almost always have more satisfying discussions, feel more confident about their decisions, and engage in more spirited debate than those groups that are plunged directly into the consensus discussion.

We believe that the brief sharing of individual perspectives enables the team to quickly assess the degree of agreement and disagreement and where specifically the most significant agreements and disagreements lie. In addition, each person is immediately heard and feels a sense of contribution to the team. They recognize that each person's view is given an equal and fair hearing before debate begins. These factors contribute to the team's ability to consider all perspectives from the outset of their discussion. When perspective taking begins early, the full examination of all viewpoints is much more likely. Teams that practice perspective taking in the face of differing opinions and ideas consistently leverage their conflicts productively.

The steps teams take and the techniques they use before conflict can help prevent harmful conflict, maintain the right climate, balance task and relationship conflict, and seize opportunities generated by conflict. These techniques are not a guarantee of conflict-free teams, and we wouldn't want them to be. Teams with foresight and a foundation of shared commitments and trust are, however, more likely to confront conflict with confidence and optimism.

## During

Clearly the bulk of the techniques we recommend are those aimed at addressing conflict as it occurs. Think of these techniques as you would a carpenter's tools. Each tool is most useful when used thoughtfully and for the right job. Many tools can be used in a variety of ways. Pliers can be used to pry a nail out of a piece of wood, twist wires together, or hold a piece of metal steady. When misused, some tools can cause irreparable damage. Have you ever drilled a hole too deep or sawed a piece of wood too short? There's an old saying that every problem looks like a nail if the only tool you have is a hammer.

In this section, we share a variety of techniques that teams can use during times of conflict. Some of the tools are easier to use than others, and a few of them may require the assistance of an expert for the best results. Just as with a carpenter's tools, wise selection and proper use of the techniques will result in the most desirable outcomes.

## Summer Before Fall

The name of this technique is a play on words. It refers to the process of *summarizing* another's view before *falling* into an explanation of one's own view. It is designed to prevent teammates who have a passionate view or position from dominating the discussion without acknowledging others' points of view.

The technique is intellectually quite easy to understand. It can be challenging to use, though, especially when debate or discussion about a conflict is heated. Any team member can initiate the use of this technique by simply asking teammates to summarize another's position, feeling, or idea before making a point. When a team has an appointed meeting facilitator, this technique can be especially valuable as a process intervention. The team leader can also use it to slow down discussions and enable deeper consideration of opposing points of view.

Remember the confusing team discussion among Dave, Cindy, Chris, and Jay at the picnic we described in Chapter Four? Imagine how the invocation of "summer before fall" might have cooled and contained their rising conflict. It doesn't matter who initiates it. In this case, watch how Jay successfully intervenes:

Dave: I'll be sure to bring the results from the client focus group meeting we have scheduled for next Monday.
Jay: That's good, Dave. We'll need those results so we can compare them to the results from the previous focus groups.

Cindy (with eyebrows raised): Aren't the results from the earlier groups old news? Those took place months ago before we included the new product's specs.

Dave: No problem. The meeting next week will include all the new specs. It wouldn't make sense to use the old model with this group.

Chris: Yeah, but unless we compare the results from before with the current group's response, what's the purpose for having our meeting?

Jay: Hey, guys, I think we need to get our summer before the fall here. Chris, your point is that comparing the views of the old focus groups with the new focus groups won't add value because the groups will be evaluating different models. Correct?

Chris: Exactly.

Jay: Okay. That makes sense. But I'm thinking we need to have comparative data from the groups to do an informed analysis.

Chris: I don't disagree. It's just that we'll need to run enough focus groups on the new model so we can do comparisons on the same data.

Dave: Right. Got it.

The technique is simple and useful. Some teams tell us that giving the technique a catchy name helps them remember to use it. It is most effective when used before teammates argue themselves into polar positions. In the case above, Jay was able to summarize Chris's thinking instead of stating his own perspective first. This brief summarization slowed the conversation and everyone's thinking down so they could consider rather than react.

When one teammate is able to restate another teammate's position or viewpoint to the satisfaction of the original speaker, good things happen. The first speaker feels acknowledged and understood. The summarizing speaker becomes mindful of the first speaker's point. The remainder of the team hears the point from a slightly different point of view and can assess it carefully. The technique is the epitome of perspective taking. When alternate perspectives are heard and understood, more possibilities for agreement are available.

## Devil's Advocacy

This technique is affectionately described by some of our colleagues as "perspective taking on steroids." It has been recognized as a tried-and-true element of problem solving for decades. In our work with teams embroiled in conflict, the act of playing devil's advocate has been useful for breaking through certain opposing hard-and-fast positions among teammates.

The technique asks those with opposing views to go beyond summarizing their conflict partners' views. It requires that the conflict partners literally argue for their opponent's position, feelings, and ideas. Negotiation expert Roger Fisher, in a 1985 video presentation of a classic negotiating simulation called HackerStar, makes the point that "if you want to change someone's mind, you first have to know where that mind is." Devil's advocacy endeavors to do exactly that: discover the perspectives, interests, and positions of one's teammates.

We have no special or privileged insight into the examples that follow. We think it is useful, though, to imagine how two similar historically significant decisions teams made may have turned out differently if devil's advocacy had been fully embraced at the time. First, what were the circumstances involved with the decision to send the cruise ship *Titanic* on her maiden voyage across the North Atlantic? Most historical accounts point to a sense of overconfidence that the ship was so structurally sound and mechanically advanced that it was virtually unsinkable. Were there other points of view? How effectively were they heard? More recently, what about the well-documented fatal decision to launch the space shuttle *Challenger* in 1986? By all accounts, the nature of the ill-fated teleconference the day before the launch was one of polarization and confrontation. The engineer from Morton Thiokol argued repeatedly that the O-rings in the booster rockets could fail at the expected low temperatures at launch time. The National Aeronautics and Space Administration (NASA) managers argued with equal passion that no scientific evidence was available to support this contention and that a delayed launch was unacceptable. The two sides became locked into their positions, and ultimately NASA decided to launch. Were the views of the Morton Thiokol engineer completely understood? Was all the available information presented and summarized? Were all options completely considered?

We don't know with certainty that the use of devil's advocacy would have had a significant impact on either decision. What we are suggesting is that the technique of arguing for an opposing position or view, and against one's own position or view, is an effective way to engage in more careful and complete consideration of the conflict. It helps maintain focus on the task conflict while resisting the plunge into relationship conflict. When used in team settings, devil's advocacy can result at least in a better appreciation of different viewpoints, if not an immediate tangible change in one's own position. This alone begins to cool the relationship conflict and enables more thoughtful, meaningful examination of the task conflict.

## Reaching Out

We have underscored the connection between task and relationship conflict at some length in this book. The technique of reaching out is focused solely on the value of maintaining and caring for the relationships among teammates during conflict. When this is done effectively, the heat generated by the opposing points of view can be held in check as the sides debate the merits of their views rather than sink into relationship-depleting accusations and assumptions.

As a technique, reaching out involves attempting to resume communicating with a conflict partner, trying to repair emotional damage caused during a conflict, and offering an apology or making amends when warranted. It is useful in one-on-one conflicts as well as in team conflicts. In team conflicts, reaching out is especially powerful when the dialogue occurs with the entire team.

We were asked to work with a highly specialized team working at a cancer research hospital. The team had been together for a number of years. The team leader role became available when the long-time leader retired. The spouse of a prominent physician at the hospital was selected as the new team leader. Although technically competent and experienced in the field, the new leader brought a very different style of leadership to the team. Almost immediately, the team members began to question her abilities, balk at her suggestions, and dismiss her attempts to improve some of the team's processes. As the months progressed, the team leader and the team found themselves at odds over even previously agreed-on procedures and work guidelines. Not only was the quality of their work suffering, but the relationships were strained to the limit. The human resource group attempted to intervene, but the team continued to flounder.

Our approach included a series of meetings, observations, assessments, and exercises, but fundamental in our intervention was addressing the stressed relationships on the team. The relationships needed to be improved, even if only slightly, for there to be any hope of progress on the business issues at hand.

Progress in our first few sessions was slow, almost imperceptible. Teammates later admitted that they behaved better than usual mostly due to the fact that we were there and they wanted to avoid embarrassment. In our third session, we provided specific observational feedback regarding the way team members interacted. We felt it appropriate to describe the interactions tactfully but with the bluntness it deserved. On hearing our perspectives, team members were sobered at the reality of their situation. Sensing their vulnerability and motivation to improve, we suggested the technique of reaching out to one another. We asked team members to think about anything they would like to say to each other about the recent decline of relationships. We invited them to share their thoughts specifically regarding how others might be feeling. The session began as follows:

Dallas: (hesitatingly) Melinda, I'm really sorry for how we've welcomed you into the team. I suppose *welcome* isn't really the right word for it.

Nancy: We didn't really give you a chance.

Melinda: (nodding slightly) Thank you.

David: You must be feeling like a complete outsider around us. What can I do to help you feel more a part of the team?

Melinda: I'm really not sure.

Dallas: I guess I didn't realize just how tough we've been on you and in some ways on ourselves. We really haven't accomplished much in the past few weeks. Do you think we can move forward from here?

O'Neil: I've probably been the worst. Sara [the former team leader] was a good friend of mine. The last thing I wanted to do was deal with a change. It didn't matter who the new leader was. I didn't want anyone else but Sara.

Nancy: I actually found myself getting upset with you at times, O'Neil. I know I wasn't easy on Melinda, but I wish I had said something to the team.

Melinda: It's been very tough, I admit. And I know I've thought some pretty terrible things about you all too.

Dallas: (chuckling) Imagine that. Why would you ever think poorly of us?

O'Neil: How can we begin to get back on the right track?

David: Maybe we should keep talking like this for awhile.

Once one person, Dallas, offered an acknowledgment of the emotional damage caused during the conflict, the rest of the team felt freer to add their own perspectives. The sheer volume of empathy, apologies, and understanding began to form a new platform from which the team could begin again. The significance of this session was profound. The challenge of having a new team leader didn't get any easier, but the choices team members began making about how to address the challenge improved dramatically. Melinda is still the team leader today, and the team is once again performing at the high levels they achieved when Sara was their leader.

## Time-Outs

In Chapter Four you read the account of a brewing conflict situation during a team presentation. James became irritated with his teammate Renee when he perceived that she failed to give his work group credit for a project. He took a personal time-out as a way to cool down his emotions and slow his response. He was able in a very short period of time to recognize his feelings, gather his thoughts, and reengage in the meeting constructively. In a similar way, teams can take a collective time-out when they encounter obstacles and challenges that stir up emotional responses and destructive interactions.

When you read the chaotic dialogue from the team attempting to resolve the nuclear waste spill earlier, did you find yourself wondering why nobody on the team asked for a time-out? Having had the advantage of seeing this exercise live, we certainly did. In fact, although we have conducted this activity hundreds of times over the years, we invariably find ourselves cringing when the communication becomes most chaotic and hoping that someone will call a time-out. Once in a while it happens. Let's take a look at how it played out for our nuclear waste disposal team. We'll rejoin them partway through their experience and follow them just a little further than before:

> S Evelyn: What should I do with Erica?
>
> S Bob: Erica just needs to stay put. We've got to get Greg farther to the right, I think. Connie, can you move Greg more that direction? (pointing)
>
> T Greg (exasperated): "This way, that way." Can't you guys just say "left" and "right"?
>
> S Connie: Hey, everyone, we have to tell our technicians "left" and "right"!
>
> T Greg: Thank you.
>
> S Connie: Make sure to listen. We've got to get this right.
>
> T Greg: You want me to move to the right?
>
> S Connie: No! Correct. Wait! I meant to say "correct," not "right." (laughing) Arrgh, this is driving me crazy!
>
> T Vanessa (standing blindfolded alone): Hello. Nobody's talking to me. Do I need to do anything?
>
> S Rick: No, you're fine.
>
> S Bob: All right, now everybody needs to begin lowering their rope very slowly.
>
> (Several technicians' voices all at once . . .)
>
> T Keith: Now?
>
> T Mark: How slowly?
>
> T Erica: How far?
>
> T Vanessa: Me too?
>
> T Greg: Memo to the supervisors: we can't see!
>
> S Bob: We understand that. You've all got to work together now. On the count of three we start lowering. One, two . . .
>
> S Evelyn: Wait! Everyone's not lowering!
>
> S Connie: Stop! Stop! We're way off-center.
>
> T Keith: Can just one person talk at a time? This is very confusing.
>
> S Bob: Yes. Good idea. Listen to my voice. We can do this. Here we go. One, two . . .

S Rick: No! No! No!

S Connie: The bucket is tilting. We're gonna lose it!

S Bob (shouting): Everybody stop!

(momentary silence)

T Keith: Is everything okay?

S Bob: Barely. The sleazium is still on the bucket but it's off-center now.

T Keith: Can I suggest that the supervisors take a minute to regroup? I mean, you guys can see what's going on. Figure out what we need to do, and then let's give it another try.

T Erica: Yeah, and we can catch our breath!

As you recall, the team was eventually successful. During our debriefing discussion, we asked the participants if they recalled any turning points or key moments in the exercise. Supervisors Bob and Connie both described the time-out as critical for the team's ultimate successful completion of the task. Bob said, "When Keith called the time-out after we had the near spill, it allowed us a chance to rethink our plan. That was huge." In Connie's words, "I agree. But it did more than that. It took the stress down a notch or two. I don't think we could have kept going without a break." Technician Erica perhaps said it best: "I remember thinking that this was just too hard. Everybody was shouting directions, telling us to do this, then that, then yelling at us to stop. When we decided to take a time-out, I was so relieved. I needed a break. I really did."

In the middle of a conflict, a time-out can serve several purposes. First, it allows the opportunity to at least temporarily escape the heat of the moment. In this case, when Keith asked for the time-out, everybody seemed to feel a sense of relief (even Tim, the facilitator merely observing the action was thankful for the break!). The team's collective frustration cooled down. Second, a time-out enables reflection and reconsideration. Keith's very words, "Can I suggest that the supervisors take a minute to regroup? I mean, you guys can see what's going on. Figure out what we need to do, and then let's give it another try," indicate the potential value of a pause or slowing the process. Finally, especially in a team context, as the personal stress and strain on individuals subside and everyone begins to reflect on what has happened and what needs to happen, the collective climate stabilizes and begins to improve. At this point, the team can begin to re-engage.

We have one final thought regarding not only this technique in particular, but for all the team techniques. In the example, Keith, a blindfolded technician, called for the time-out. Often such procedural suggestions in this exercise, and in reality, are left to those assumed to have the power, authority, or, as in this case, vision. Part of the power of using time-outs is that anybody on the team can call for one. Team members don't have to wait for the team leader or more influential members. Every teammate has the power, and the responsibility, to use this tool. We suggest that all teams create an agreement or norm that expressly encourages this responsibility.

## Reframing Through Inquiry

One of the characteristics of conflict is how quickly disagreements over content issues (task conflict) can become entangled with interpersonal issues (relationship conflict). This can occur in the blink of an eye and without notice by team members. What was in one moment a hearty debate over the future options for new business development morphs into an argument over who has the better track record for attracting new clients. One level of protection against such problems is the technique or art of reframing.

Some people we have observed and with whom we have worked seem to have a knack for reframing. The kind of reframing we're talking about is reframing with the intent to clarify or reexamine for better understanding. There is also a type of reframing that is used with the sole intent of redirecting discussions to topics or issues of the speaker's choice. There are certainly times and places for this type of reframing. We wish, however, to focus on the use of reframing for addressing team conflict. In particular, we suggest that the best way to use this tool is through inquiry versus advocacy, questions versus statements. Thus, we refer to it as reframing through inquiry.

In his award-winning training video *Everyday Creativity*, narrator and world-renowned photographer Dewitt Jones makes the case for reframing problems and obstacles into opportunities (Jones, 1999). Using examples from his portfolio, Jones demonstrates how several photographs he took that didn't quite measure up to his standards left him frustrated about how to improve his results. One photo shows a wispy spider web in a tree in the early morning dawn. Another photo shows a wildflower against a backdrop of green grasses. Yet another depicts the image of a young girl sleeping in a shade-covered hammock. To the untrained observer (like us), each photo looks pretty darn good. But to Jones, each represents an opportunity for something better, something more in line with his vision and purpose. As his presentation continues, he shows several more photos of the same subjects from slightly altered points of view. He changes lenses, switches his perspective, shoots from different angles, and suddenly the new photos take the viewer to a whole new level. The photo of the spider web is now a close-up view that allows the observation of dew drops on the slender threads of silk, sunlight glinting through the drops, and the spider itself perched at the edge of the web. The new photo of the wildflower is now framed against the image of an old barn in the background and with bits of blue sky above. The photo of the little girl shows only her tender face pressed peacefully against the weave of the rope hammock, thick eyelashes resting as she naps in the breeze of a lazy summer afternoon. Then Jones reveals that the little girl is his daughter and that regardless of his reframing, he thinks she looks good no matter how he sees her.

Our simple written descriptions do little justice to the beauty of Jones's actual photos. We are in awe of his work. And the point he makes about reframing is masterfully clear: when we don't give up on problems and issues and reframe them instead, they become opportunities.

Applying this technique intellectually to conflict in teams is hardly a stretch. Implementing it, actually doing it, can be a bit more of a challenge, especially when you are in the middle of a conflict with your colleagues. The specific technique for reframing that we advocate uses well-timed inquiries about the topic, process, assumptions, or progress of the team.

Obviously each situation and each team calls for a slightly unique approach for reframing with questions. The team member doing the reframing must accurately refer to the current situation when posing the question or making the inquiry. It is important also that the questions and inquiries are posed with nonthreatening language and delivery. For instance, in the middle of an intense team debate, rather than ask a teammate, "Why do you keep saying that?" it may be more useful to frame the question as, "I'm not sure why you're saying that. Can you help me understand?" Here are some examples that illustrate the nature of this tool:

- What might be the consequences of that course of action?
- What if we found our assumption to be in error?
- Are there more than just these two alternatives?
- What else might we try?
- Please help me understand why.
- You obviously see it differently. I'd like to hear you say more.
- How important is this versus that?
- How does this discussion fit with our main priority?
- What impact will our decision on this topic have on . . .?
- Will spending more time now on this pay off on that?
- What would it take to change your [or our] minds?
- Would it be helpful to revisit what we've already decided or know?

As you can imagine, the use of reframing can be one of the most valuable tools in a conflict competent team's toolbox. Reframing requires tact, skill, and good timing. The most obvious times to engage in it are also among the most difficult and risky. One common purpose of reframing is to unlock discussions that have become entrenched as participants take and defend positions. As the deliberation heats up, the discussion often becomes characterized by more and more frequent statements and assertions. It becomes tempting even for the well-meaning intervening teammate to declare what should happen ("We have to stop bickering and move on!") rather than inquire about the options ("What can we do to break the stalemate?")

The technique of reframing through inquiry enables teams to seize opportunities presented by conflict. Options for addressing tough and touchy disagreements are more often found by asking the right questions than driving for the right answers.

## Brainstorming

Brainstorming has long been a tool for problem solving. The value of creating multiple options for consideration is unquestioned for addressing complex, difficult challenges. In the same way, teams that routinely consider multiple options and alternatives seem to have fewer incidents of interpersonal conflict (Eisenhardt, Kahwajy, and Bourgeois, 1997b).

Take a minute to recall times when you and your team were engaged in your most significant problem-solving or decision-making conflicts. What were the circumstances? More important, what options were you debating? Even more specifically, how many options were under consideration? Our bet is that in many cases of significant team conflict, the team was focused on just one or two alternatives. When the options are so limited, it is easier for the conflict to become more personal and heated. Teammates begin taking sides in the debate, positions are staked out, and the decision quickly can be perceived as a win-lose proposition. In contrast, when teams consider multiple options, debate is unbounded because choices aren't limited to either this or that. Teammates are free to consider and integrate perspectives and ideas from several sources rather than lock in on a single idea. The resulting discussion is one of exploration rather than exclusion.

Teams can apply this same notion as a tool for maneuvering through conflict. Al, Scott, Ed, Jamie, and Andy work in the marketing group for a large telecommunications company. The company's network had experienced some recent technical difficulties, resulting in the disruption of service for thousands of customers in a major metropolitan area. The team was locked in a fiery debate about how to restore customer confidence in their service. Let's pick up the conversation during the middle of a meeting where they were under significant time pressure for making decisions about their approach:

> Scott: Look, we have to go right back after them [their clients]. We can't hold back. We apologize, we credit their accounts, and we move on.
>
> Al: I couldn't agree more. That's what I've been saying all along. There's only one way to deal with a problem like this: you have to get over it quickly and move ahead.
>
> Andy: Guys, I just don't buy it. It's more complex that that. Our customers need more than just an apology and a credit. They want something more than a business-as-usual attitude from us.
>
> Jamie: I have to agree with Andy. It's going to take some finesse to win them back. I think your approach is just too simple.
>
> Al (sounding irritated): I've been around for a lot longer than any of you. You've got to trust me on this. The longer we finesse the issue, the longer our customers will remember the problem and the more likely they are never to forgive us.
>
> Scott: Al is right. He's been through this kind of thing before.
>
> Ed: I don't know what to think. I do know we have to come up with something quick, or all our butts are on the line.
>
> Jamie: That's for sure. Why don't we vote? Do we go for a quick fix like Al and Scott propose? Or do we create a campaign that wins back as much confidence as possible over a period of time?

Al: Wait a minute! I object to your characterization of our plan. It's not just a quick fix. We'll take a comprehensive approach. We just can't drag it out with a campaign, for goodness sake.

Scott: Yeah! That's not fair.

Andy: Calm down, you two! Ed is more right than any of us. We're all going to be in big trouble if we don't have a proposal for Joe [their boss] by Friday.

Scott (sighing loudly): Well, what do we do now?

Jamie (looking around the team): Let's vote.

Ed (speaking slowly): Gentleman, a vote puts me right on the bubble. I don't like that. And frankly, I don't want that kind of pressure. I have another idea. Why don't we agree that these two approaches are possibilities and try to come up with some more possibilities?

Al (sarcastically): Here we go.

Andy: How would that work?

Ed: Well, we just stop debating these two ideas and try to come up with some other ideas.

Scott: But I like Al's and my idea.

Jamie: Andy and I like ours too. But that's not helping us make any progress. We've been stuck for the last hour.

Scott: True. We're making no headway.

Ed: So what do you say? Is it worth a try?

Jamie: I don't see how it could hurt.

Andy: Okay by me.

Al: Fine, but I don't think this is going to change my mind.

Scott: Let's give it a whirl.

Ed: Great.

Even though they started slowly, the team came up with seven new ideas over the next fifteen minutes. Several were variations on the two original suggestions. Others were novel and offered slightly different ways of thinking about the problem. In addition, the fifteen minutes spent not focused exclusively on the two original ideas provided a sense of relief for all the team members. Ultimately the team agreed on a proposal that incorporated the swift action Al and Scott advocated with the creation of a marketing campaign similar to the ideas Jamie and Andy originally advocated: the campaign touted the history of innovation and service provided by the company rather than focusing on the recent problem. This idea surfaced during the brief brainstorming session and proved to be instrumental in enabling the team to return to problem solving rather than debating the merits of their seemingly mutually exclusive ideas.

Brainstorming is a technique most teams easily embrace and want to use for addressing their conflicts. Remember, though, the suggestions made earlier: when the only tool you carry is a hammer, you may treat every problem like a nail. Brainstorming is a valuable tool, but the most conflict competent teams have a toolbox containing many tools. We recommend that you and your team learn how to use all the tools available so you'll have more options for addressing conflict most effectively.

## Observing

The technique of observation may seem somehow strange or out of place for addressing conflict on teams. "How," you may ask, "can observing alone possibly help my team handle conflict more effectively?" The answer is that observing alone probably will not have much permanent impact, although in our years of working with teams, we have found in the vast majority of cases that the actual behavior of team members appears more effective than when described in advance. We can recall more than a few cases when we were prepared and expecting to see disastrous team meetings, only to be surprised by civility and cooperation. Industrial psychologists noticed and documented this phenomenon years ago and refer to it as the Hawthorne effect. In short, when people know they are being observed, they temporarily change, and often improve, their behavior and productivity. The technique of observation suggested here however, goes beyond the simple, isolated act of observation. When an observer watches, records, and provides feedback on what he or she sees, there is great opportunity for understanding what behaviors or processes are interfering with the team's ability to handle conflict.

This technique is well suited for assistance by an expert or outside resource. We discuss two approaches suggesting that a team member or an outside resource serve as the observer. There are several reasons to use an outside resource or expert. First, an expert is trained in this kind of group observation and is more likely to spot more behaviors and identify them accurately. Second, when a team member is designated as the observer, the true team dynamics are altered. Third, an outside resource may be perceived as more objective in his or her perceptions than any team member acting as an observer. When selecting this tool, we encourage teams to consider the merits of using an outside resource versus a current team member for the role of observer.

There are at least two ways the technique of observing can work. First, one person is designated as the team's observer. The task is to watch and make notes about specific behaviors of team members. This technique works best with teams that have had a shared experience in a training program or with assessment instruments that have provided them a common language for labeling conflict behaviors. The Conflict Dynamics Profile (CDP) assessment instrument, described earlier, is one such tool. An observer can effectively create a checklist using the seven constructive and eight destructive scales identified in the CDP. With the checklist in hand, the observer can easily record instances of team members' behaviors by checking them off as they occur.

The team may decide to take several time-outs during the meeting so the observer can provide feedback about the behaviors noted. This technique is somewhat disruptive to the flow of the meeting, but it has the benefit of enabling team members to alter their behaviors in a more immediate way. When waiting until after the meeting, the observer reports on the volume of each kind of behavior witnessed, as well as comments on the impact of those behaviors. The value of such an approach is maximized when the team immediately discusses the results and commits to changing behaviors that are problematic and continuing behaviors that are constructive.

A second approach is similar but fully incorporates a real-time element. Like the first, this approach also works best when a common understanding and language regarding communication and conflict exists among all team members. The task of the observer is not only to identify the behaviors noticed, but to label them aloud during the meeting. This real-time feedback makes it extraordinarily clear to the participants when constructive or destructive behaviors are being used. In our experience, this approach is very effective when used in training or exercise settings. Because the nature of the techniques requires the observer to call out behaviors, some team members may find it too disconcerting for use in actual team meetings. Regardless of the setting, this technique powerfully recognizes specific behaviors and interactions that have a constructive or destructive impact on the team's ability to handle conflict.

Our good friend Sherod Miller has developed a system for observing by using a process called *mapping an issue*. The process helps team members monitor their conversation, then work through complicated conflicted issues. Miller's approach is flexible enough to accommodate both in-the-moment identification of constructive and destructive behaviors and after-the-interaction discussion of behaviors that enables collaborative outcomes. He teaches this process in the revised Collaborative Team Skills program (Miller, 2007).

The discussion of this technique usually results in questions about the usefulness of videotaping. We are major proponents of videotaping as a tool in assessing and improving a team's conflict competence. We will discuss the use of videotaping in more depth in the section of this chapter referring to techniques best positioned after the conflict.

## Clearing the Air (Safely)

In Chapter Four we discussed the merits of using constructive communication skills and behaviors. One of the key behaviors we cited was expressing emotions. The challenge of doing so effectively lies in one's ability to manage the experiencing of strong emotions while honestly describing those emotions to others. The technique of clearing the air safely offers teams a method for expressing emotions in a somewhat structured way. This technique is most applicable when conflicting views have resulted in overt displays of emotion or in suspected covert masking of feelings among team members.

Let's revisit the difficulty the selection team at the large conference center experienced while trying to make a hiring decision. The team consisted of Mike, Becky, Sue, Murray and Jerry. They were discussing three finalists, Luke, Taylor, and Brice, for the position of manager of conference services. We focused in this case primarily on Jerry's inability to express his emotions to the rest of the team. Now let's consider the entire team and how well or poorly they communicated about thoughts and feelings with one another. We will pick up their conversation shortly before they decided to take a break:

> Becky: Jerry, I'm going to go out a limb here. I don't think you were happy when we eliminated Luke. Is that right?
> (Jerry tilts his head slightly and raises an eyebrow but doesn't say anything.)
> Becky: I noticed that you haven't said anything or asked any questions while we've debated Taylor and Brice.
> Mike: Are you upset that we dropped Luke?
> Sue: Do you think that was a bad call?
> Jerry: It doesn't matter. It was a team decision.
> Murray: Of course, it matters. We all want to make the best decision. If you're holding back, it's not fair to the team.

You may have thoughts or feelings that we haven't considered.

Jerry: I think the best course of action is to abide by the decisions we've already made. My feelings aren't hurt.

Sue: So you didn't want to eliminate Luke.

Jerry (beginning to sound irritated): Look, can we just forget Luke? We need to decide between the remaining two.

Mike: Maybe we should take a quick break first. I know I could use one.

Jerry: Fine. Let's come back in ten minutes.

The team members silently left the conference room. Mike and Sue ducked into Sue's office while Becky and Murray walked to the break room. As soon as he shut the door to Sue's office, Mike said, "Do you believe him? Why is he so afraid to admit that he's upset with our decision?" Sue nodded in agreement: "He's acting the way he always does. He never offers any clue as to how he's thinking during these kinds of meetings. It really ticks me off." Across the office in the break room, Becky was pouring a cup of coffee and said to Murray, "What is up with Jerry? If he's surprised at our thoughts about Luke, why doesn't he just say so?" Murray thought for a moment, then said, "Sometimes I think we're too tough on Jerry. These are critical decisions, and I'm sure he just wants to make sure we weighed all the evidence." Meanwhile Jerry walks toward his office. As he passes by Darcy, his assistant, he remarks just loud enough for her to hear, "I don't know why I trusted them with this decision in the first place."

Do you notice any strong thoughts and feelings? Everyone on the team has them. Most of the focus is on Jerry's behavior. It seemed obvious to the team that he was holding back. But the team members were not exactly straight with Jerry or each other during the meeting. Once they decided to break, however, the emotions flowed frequently and easily. Might there have been another alternative, a better way to share those thoughts and feelings that could lead to more satisfying and productive inter-actions? We think so.

The team, not just Jerry, can benefit by temporarily paus-ing their discussion about the candidates and focusing on their interpersonal communication—or in this case, their lack of communication. Any team member can call for a time-out and suggest that they clear the air. What is required is that each team member identifies his or her thoughts and feelings about the nature of the discussion and then honestly commu-nicates those thoughts and feelings to the others.

The process can have a little to a lot of structure. Structure can be added by asking team members to first write down words that describe their current feelings. Next, team members are asked to identify the source of those feelings. We recommend that at least one source is owned by or in the control of the writer. Finally, next to each source, the person lists alternatives that may have resulted in a different reaction or response. The alternatives must include information about the source and one-self. For example, let's look at what Sue may have written.

*Current feelings:* frustration and anger

*Sources:* (1) Jerry is holding back, again! (2) I'm not helping him communicate.

*Alternatives:* (1) Jerry should admit when he sees something dif-ferently. (2) I should ask him more questions and tell him that I'm really interested in his thoughts.

Once all team members have completed their lists, they take turns sharing their thoughts and feelings. This technique and the structure surrounding it provide support for engaging in the effective expression of emotions. It also creates a safe way to communicate about the emotions that are invariably generated during debates and deliberations.

Had this team engaged in the straight talk involved in clearing the air before they took the break, they may have been in a better position to continue their critical hiring decision afterward. Not only would they have understood the others' views and feelings better, they would have avoided the damaging off-line discussions in Sue's office and the break room. Darcy, Jerry's assistant, would also have been spared Jerry's under-his-breath demeaning comments regarding the rest of the team.

Clearing the air requires courage and honesty. It is risky business to admit strong emotions. It's also risky, if following the structure presented above, to present alternative suggestions to your teammates. These risks make it prudent to again consider inviting a third-party facilitator to help with the process of clearing the air. Many organizations have representatives in HR, training, or organizational development departments who can help. Regardless of how the technique is facilitated, when teammates are honest, open, and straight with each other, bonds of trust and respect grow immeasurably. When they're not, the very foundation of the team's existence can be threatened.

## Stop, Start, Continue

This tool is one of our very favorite ways of helping teams experiencing conflict slow down so they consider what is working, what is not working, and what else is needed for improved interactions and results. We've placed this technique in the "during conflict" category because of its value in addressing troubling conflicts that shut down team effectiveness. However, it can just as easily be used in the "after conflict" category as a way of debriefing conflict situations that have been resolved so teams can apply their experience to future challenges.

This tool bears the name "Stop, Start, Continue." It's a nice name. It even has a kind of catchy, alliterative ring to it. In practice though, we recommend a different sequence to the three elements. In most cases, we address them as (1) Continue, (2) Stop, and

(3) Start. It is our experience that beginning by focusing on what's working leads to a more productive conversation.

We recommend that this technique always be facilitated by someone with expertise in group dynamics. Although the process itself is not terribly complex, the notion of having the team leader or a team member facilitate the process has little attraction. As in earlier techniques, we think altering the group dynamics by removing a member has way too many downsides. In addition, this is a thorough process and can be lengthy. We conduct the process in three stages. In many cases, we schedule meeting times stretching over two different days.

The process begins by assembling the team in a private space equipped with enough tables and chairs to accommodate all team members. Whiteboards or flip charts are needed to record the large amount of data that will be created. The facilitator briefly describes the process as a way for the team to first describe how they've been dealing with their conflict, second to analyze their behaviors, and third to agree on how to address the conflict moving forward. It's important to emphasize that team members focus on sharing their ideas and perspectives openly and honestly. Keeping information and views hidden will stifle the process and prevent the team from making progress.

Stage 1 begins by seeking suggestions for what the team should continue to do in regard to the conflict it is facing. Each suggestion is recorded publicly in a way that all members can see. We prefer the use of flip charts, although higher-tech options exist. When teams have trouble getting started, we remind them that suggestions for this category can focus on what they do before, during, and after confronting the conflict. They should not limit their thinking to the time when they are actually embroiled in it. By beginning with the category Continue, teams are able to consider behaviors and interactions that have been effective, and this focus on positives provides reinforcement and recognition. It also highlights the fact that the team regularly engages in constructive behavior. In other words, although this technique addresses a problem, the team can clearly see that all is not lost. The process resembles brainstorming in that no suggestions are debated at this time. They are simply recorded.

Once the list for Continue is exhausted, the same approach is used to record suggestions for Stop. This phase is usually a bit more contentious. As team members reflect on past experiences that have not gone well, it's easy for some items to contain perspectives that seem judgmental or focused on individuals. It is important that the facilitator help maintain order at this point by recommending that observations describe behavior, not people. The listing continues until the team has difficulty coming up with additional items.

Finally, the team considers the Start category. The focus here is on what the team can do differently or better in the future. Once again, effective brainstorming rules are enforced, with no discussion or debate allowed. In many cases, Start items are reverse characterizations of items listed in the Stop category. We are generally supportive of this practice because it emphasizes the need for change. Of course, independent suggestions also make the list. If the team has difficulty, the facilitator can suggest that they scan the previously created Continue list, a practice that often results in ideas for building on behaviors and processes already seen as worthwhile.

Once all three categories are addressed, we suggest taking a break. During this time, all responses are displayed, and team members are asked to review each list. Each team member carries a notepad for jotting down additional suggestions for the lists. After the break, these new suggestions are recorded.

We find that many teams have a feeling of accomplishment at this point in the process. As team members look around the meeting room, they see the walls covered with data on the flip charts that they created. The sheer volume of information alone gives team members the sense that they have made progress and that much more is possible. Capitalizing on this sense of accomplishment is the goal of the next stage.

In stage 2, the team members review each category. They discuss the items and agree on suggestions for the team to continue, to cease, or to begin. The methodology for stage 2 can take a variety of forms and may include a number of process options. The ultimate goal is to clarify each item and determine whether it should stay on the list. During this stage, a number of actions can occur. For instance, we often suggest that team members consider each item by providing examples of when the action or behavior was observed and how it affected the team. This practice helps the team verify the item's value and understand its application. Another process option is grouping similar items together. This enables the team to more effectively compare items and consider the relative value of all the suggestions. These steps result in a methodical reduction of the number of suggestions and items in each category and leads to the third and final stage of this technique.

Stage 3 is a final review of each category and some prioritization of the remaining suggestions. The method and outcome for each of the categories are slightly different. In the Continue category, we often ask team members to identify the most important items to continue. One way to do so is by giving each member an opportunity to identify their personal top three or top five. As each team member reveals his or her selections, the items most important to the team become apparent. For the Stop category, the process is quite similar: team members consider each item and identify those they believe will have the most critical impact if stopped on the team's ability to handle the conflict. This method results in a clear list of things the team agrees it must stop doing.

The suggested method for considering items in the Start category is a bit more involved. Here we want the team not only to decide which actions are most important; we want them to discuss how each action will be implemented. The discussion of implementation is critical. We advocate reaching agreement on four factors: who, what, when, and how. Team members should specify *who* has responsibility for engaging in the behavior (in the vast majority of circumstances, all team members share this responsibility). This emphasizes that every team member has the authority to intervene or make suggestions when conflict occurs. The team should also consider *what* should be said or done when accessing each item on the list. This sometimes results in the identification of catchphrases that signal the team to slow down. Next, the team should consider *when*, or under what conditions, they will engage in the new behavior or process. Finally, the team discusses *how* such interventions should take place. In other words, this discussion focuses on the use of respectful, well-intentioned interventions, even when the suggestion may at first appear as an interruption. When team members agree on new specific behaviors, actions, and processes for addressing their conflict, they are well on their way to not only resolving the current conflict, but confidently handling similar conflicts in the future.

## Mediation

When task conflict morphs into relationship conflict, the rising heat of conflict is unmistakable. If unchecked, the conflict can grow in size and intensity so that it virtually engulfs the team and can become the team's primary focus. The conflict can reach Discord and Polarization levels of intensity. When it does, relationship conflict is far more obvious and harmful than task conflict. We have presented a variety of team examples that illustrate how teams have met the challenges of conflict. We hope these examples have provided glimpses into the workings of teams like yours, resulting in a sense of confidence that you too can deal with conflict competently.

Now we present a real-world example of mediation: the brewing team conflict encountered by the National Hockey League's (NHL) 2004 Stanley Cup Champion, the Tampa Bay Lightning. The team's general manager, Jay Feaster, was gracious enough to describe how the team handles conflict and share this extraordinary example of how mediation helped resolve a critical, potentially franchise-altering issue just a few years before the team's championship season. The conflict, as you will see, involved the way the team handled one of the league's rising superstar players, the contentious relationship between the player and the head coach, and the resulting impact on the team as impressions formed, factions began to develop, and the team's performance began to suffer. Although the context is a professional sports team, the conflict presented a significant challenge to the business and management of the organization. Just as in your businesses and organizations, team conflict can ultimately threaten the results necessary to compete and survive.

For readers unfamiliar with hockey, many believe it may be the most emotional of the major professional team sports. The game is characterized by virtually nonstop action, hard hitting, and intense effort. In this low-scoring game, every goal is celebrated by the entire team. Teamness is so important to the game that assists and goals are of equal value in determining a player's point total for the season. In other words, the one or two teammates who help the player who actually scores a goal are given the same amount of credit as the goal scorer. Although individual effort is often highlighted on the evening news, hockey is an absolutely team-centered game. When a conflict or other threat to the team's climate is presented, it is critical that it is addressed swiftly and effectively.

In midseason 2000–2001, the Lightning hired John Tortorella to take over as head coach for a team with a core of young stars. The future had promise if the team could capitalize on its raw skill and ability and play with a team concept that leveraged that ability. One of the brightest young talents on the team, Vincent Lecavalier, was touted as a future NHL superstar. The previous team owner, general manager, and coaching staff had held Vinny in such high regard that some of his teammates questioned his status and treatment. Vinny was named team captain at the age of nineteen, an unprecedented move by NHL standards. The pressure to perform mounted on the young phenomenon. When Tortorella took over as coach, a new era of fairness and objectivity began: playing time was earned based on performance, and excuses were not tolerated. Players were expected to play within the team concept.

In the first several months of Coach Tortorella's tenure, Vinny saw his playing time reduced. His position of playing "the point" on power plays (akin to quarterbacking a football team or playing point guard on a basketball team) was removed. Even his prime parking place in the team lot was taken away. It was clear that young Vinny and his new head coach were not seeing eye-to-eye. The young player's confidence was shaken, and he questioned his future with the team. Other teammates took notice, and slowly but surely some factions began to form.

Early the next season, Vinny and the Lightning could not agree on his contract. He held out during training camp while his agent and the Lightning management negotiated his deal. Finally, the contract was settled, and Vinny rejoined the team just before the regular season began. He did not play the first few games due to his conditioning and started the season slowly. In addition, during the off-season, several veteran players were added to the team to provide leadership and experience. Vinny was removed as team captain, and Dave Andreychuk was named new captain. Vinny's perception was that he was no longer valued by the head coach and that his status as a respected teammate was in jeopardy. Players were concerned and found it more and more difficult to know how to support everyone's best interests. Finally, Lecavalier's agent called Lightning general manager, Rick Dudley, with the simple message that Vinny could no longer play for Coach Tortorella.

Dudley, like so many of us, tended to avoid conflict. As the rift between player and coach widened and deepened, Dudley's hope that they would work it out on their own slowly vanished. By the time the request for a trade was made, the entire Lightning organization was completely frustrated. Dudley resigned. His departure illustrates perfectly the kind of far-reaching damage a conflict handled poorly between two members of a team can have on others.

Jay Feaster, the Lightning's assistant general manager, stepped into the role of general manager. He also inherited the ever swirling conflict between the head coach and the team's franchise player. By now, the impact on the rest of the team was becoming more obvious: more members of the organization began taking sides, the delicate balance of teamness continued to wobble, and the team's performance was inconsistent. But most of all, players, staff, and team executives were understandably weary of the situation. Something had to be done.

Feaster had three options. He could fire Tortorella and preserve the team's relationship with Lecavalier, who was virtually certain to be a star player for years. He could trade Lecavalier and support Coach Tortorella's style and team concept. Despite this single issue, Tortorella's approach was already showing promise. Or he could find a way to work things out among Tortorella, Lecavalier, and the team. Feaster chose to find a way.

First, he scheduled individual meetings with Vinny and the coach. He began by telling Vinny, "It is not going to be my legacy that I was the general manager that traded Vincent Lecavalier." He assured Vinny that his place with the team was secure and the future of the Lightning was bright, and that he was confident that the issues with the head coach and the team could be handled.

Next he met with Coach Tortorella. He started by stating simply, "Torts, I am not going to fire you." They spoke in general terms about how the conflict centering on Lecavalier could be addressed. Feaster and Tortorella both have young families, and they discussed the analogy of how they dealt with their own children. Feaster said, "We don't dump our child on the neighbor's doorstep when we get frustrated." In other words, the team wasn't going to trade away this problem. Tortorella agreed but maintained that the team was more important than individuals. Feaster agreed.

Feaster thought it best to allow some time to pass after the individual meetings. He did not want to appear to impose his will on either his coach or star player. He hoped that things would improve, but he knew that he couldn't allow the relationship to simmer without progress. The delicate balance on the ice and in the locker room was too precious to risk. As the season progressed, the tension didn't dramatically worsen or improve. It was time for the next step.

Feaster scheduled the first three-way meeting with Tortorella and Lecavalier. He reminded both of the commitments made during the earlier individual discussions: no trades and no firings were on the table. Jay looked both men in the eye and said, "For the good of the Lightning, we have to talk this out." During the next several meetings, both men recounted their perspectives. Feaster insisted that both listen completely to each other's views. In the end, it was clear to the player that the coach had nothing but the best interests of the team in mind. The coach understood that the player only wanted to contribute in every way he could to ensure that the team performed at the highest level. They agreed that in the best interest of the team, they had to handle their differences in ways that would not affect the others. Thus began a new relationship, still tumultuous at times, but with the understanding that they and the team were in this together.

Feaster's office became known as the "safe room." When conflicts arose that the team couldn't handle alone, players and coaches knew that they could engage in completely open, honest, frank discussions in the safe room without fear of retribution. Over the next few years, Feaster hosted a number of similar meetings. There was even another meeting with Vinny and Tortorella. Each time Feaster provided a safe environment where conflicting parties could air their differences, listen to the other perspectives, and find a way to prevail over the issues, not each other.

When we asked Feaster to summarize his philosophy of conflict management, he counted off three things. First, "Hit it head on." The longer you allow conflict to fester, the more likely it is to infect the entire team. Second, he recommended "getting everyone involved." Hockey is a team sport; it can't be played successfully any other way. In the example here, much emphasis was placed on the interaction between Coach Tortorella and Vincent Lecavalier. However, after the safe room meetings, both the coach and the player made it clear to the rest of the team that the team always comes first. Feaster encouraged this approach and offered his full assistance and support in maintaining the team concept. Finally, Feaster emphasized that the only way to make progress during conflict was to provide the opportunity for "total honesty." In his experience, the only time mediation efforts can fail is when one party holds back, avoids, or refuses to engage.

At Lightning headquarters in Tampa, Florida, the concept of Feaster's office as the safe room has become part of the fabric of the team concept. Though not infallible, mediation has proven to be a powerful technique for resolving even the toughest conflicts in the emotionally charged, high-stakes environment of a National Hockey League team. Feaster can recall only two examples of unsuccessful mediation. One incident involved a player who refused to engage honestly, or "put it on the table." The other involved an assistant coach who constantly avoided the open, frank discussion of differing coaching styles during the mediation sessions. Both the player and the assistant coach have left the Lightning organization.

We believe mediation, used judiciously, can work for any team just as effectively as it has for the Tampa Bay Lightning. The same basic tenets Jay Feaster described for resolving difficult conflicts can work for your teams too:

1. The mediation efforts are conducted in a safe environment.
2. The mediator presents ground rules that ensure safety, honesty, openness, and commitment to listening by all parties.
3. The conflict parties agree to air their views honestly and listen completely to the other views.
4. The parties agree to continue talking until progress is made.

Coach John Tortorella still leads the Lightning. He is among the longest tenured coaches in the league and has been honored as the NHL's Coach of the Year. In addition to the championship season in 2004, the club is now considered one of the perennial favorites in the NHL. Vinny Lecavalier remains with the Lightning. He led the league in scoring in 2006–2007 with fifty-two goals. A fifty-goal season is considered a rare accomplishment. Perhaps more important, he demonstrated his value as a complete team player by recording more assists than goals (a total of fifty-six assists) to set a team record of 108 points for the season. And when asked about his individual achievements, Vinny always credits his team-mates for providing him the opportunities. He now serves, in yet another display of true team spirit, with teammates Brad Richards and Martin St. Louis as one of three assistant captains.

The relationship between Tortorella and Lecavalier has continued to mature. Tortorella sees Vinny as one of the key team leaders on and off the ice. Vinny understands and supports the coach's emphasis on the team and has come to appreciate his coaching style. As of the time of this writing, the team is at the midpoint of the 2007–2008 season and battling for the division lead. Vinny is leading the league in scoring, and Coach Tortorella is touting him as the league's most valuable player. Optimism runs high. The team's strength lies not only in its hockey skills but in their faith and trust in one another.

Perhaps the key to successful team conflict mediation is best summed up in a phrase that is heard often in Lightning player and coach interviews. It seems to echo through the halls of the Tampa Bay locker room and general offices, especially when the team suffers a tough loss or is about to face a stiff challenge. "We've got to find a way," say members of the Lightning. That same attitude and mind-set can enable team members on any team to confront conflict confidently through the technique of mediation.

## Using These Tools

The ten techniques we have presented for consideration during conflict can help teams when they are stuck. Conflict can, and will, cause even the most highly functioning teams to resort to destructive and ineffective approaches. These tools work best when used in concert with constructive communication skills and behaviors. However, they are most often accessed when a team's communication ability is most challenged. Never assume that these techniques can take the place of constructive communication skills or the maintenance of a trusting, productive team climate. Use them wisely, and you will find that even the most difficult conflicts are possible to resolve. In the process, your team will continue to gain confidence for engaging the inevitable conflicts lurking in the future.

## After

Many world-class teams regularly review both the accomplishment of their goals and milestones and their swings and misses. This process helps teams evaluate not only their pure results, but the behaviors, tactics, and ideas that worked, whether or not the results were perfect. Think of the times a colleague has given her best effort but failed to produce the desired result. For instance, even the most polished presenter may fail to persuade an audience to embrace the merits of a new idea. It is equally important for teams as a whole to assess the effectiveness of their efforts related to team conflict. Teams must look not only at their track record of resolving conflicts, but how they've addressed conflicts when they occur. Both techniques we recommend leverage the concept of conducting thorough, honest reviews of what's worked well or not so well after a conflict has been resolved.

### Periodic Peer Feedback

Team members are in the unique position of working hand-in-hand with colleagues to accomplish shared goals. They build working relationships that are characterized not only by proximity but, in the best cases, by mutually satisfying interactions that lead to trust and collaboration. Even when the teammates don't forge friendships outside of work, they still rely on each other to communicate clearly and honestly about their shared projects. It is this spirit of clear, honest communication that enables team members to provide ongoing feedback to one another about the nature of their interactions.

Teams performing at the highest levels integrate ongoing feedback among members as part of their routine communication. They share feedback about miscommunications and misunderstandings that occur during work in real time. They also provide reinforcing feedback in the same way. This level of consistent, ongoing, integrated team feedback is a lofty standard. The technique of periodic peer feedback can help teams commit to engaging in this kind of dialogue on a consistent, if not fully integrated, basis.

We recommend that teams set aside times for conducting peer feedback sessions. The model we advocate is similar to the process we use in many of our multiday leadership and team development programs at the Leadership Development Institute. During these programs, learning teams are formed to participate in several problem-solving exercises and simulations. Team members are asked to observe each other's actions while participating in these activities so they can provide feedback to one another later during the program. Often we teach a model for observing and providing feedback to provide a format or framework. One useful model is the situation-behavior-impact (SBI) approach:

*Situation:* The context in which the behavior or action took place

*Behavior:* What was said or done

*Impact:* The impact of the behavior on the observer or others in the situation

After spending several days together in one of these highly interactive programs, team members have observed an enormous amount of behavior—so much so that we must carefully monitor the amount of time spent sharing feedback with each individual on the team so every team member has an equal opportunity for receiving feedback. Considering the volume of feedback accumulated during a week-long training program, imagine the amount of information each of your teammates has about each other after working together for months, even years.

To be most effective, the technique of periodic peer feedback requires some structure. The SBI model provides a degree of structure. It is an excellent framework for sharing behavioral feedback with teammates. In addition, when facilitating peer feedback sessions for teams, we recommend several other steps and guidelines:

1. Conduct the session away from potential interruptions and distractions.

2. Depending on the size of the team, set a reasonable time period for the session. For teams of five to seven members, two hours is recommended.

3. Team members should come prepared with SBI observations for each teammate.

4. Each team member should request feedback by asking teammates to share their observations.

5. To ensure safety, team members can pass on providing or requesting feedback.

6. Each team member takes a turn on the "receiving seat." When a team member asks for feedback, all other team members provide SBI observations in turn.

7. While receiving feedback, the receiver does not defend or explain but simply listens and takes notes if he or she wishes.

8. Once all the feedback is shared, the receiver may ask clarifying questions, again without defending or explaining.

9. The receiver thanks all the teammates, and the process continues until all members have a chance on the receiving seat.

For some teams, it may be valuable to incorporate a facilitator to assist with these sessions. This is especially true for teams that have experienced frequent or severe conflict recently. It's also a good idea for teams that have never tried this technique in the past. Ultimately most teams can manage these sessions on their own and find them to be valuable, fulfilling experiences.

Certainly teams don't have to wait for a resolution of a conflict to engage in this technique. Although we placed this technique in the "after conflict" category, it can be an effective tool for reviewing team interactions any time during the team's life span. The more teammates communicate with each other about what is working and what can be improved, the more likely it is that conflicts can be handled at the lower levels of intensity. When this happens, teams consistently enjoy the benefits of conflict while reducing the harmful effects of conflict gone bad.

## "Reviewing the Tape"

This technique uses a specific behavior and process review in the aftermath of a team conflict. Unlike the periodic peer review technique, this tool enables the team to look back on a specific conflict situation to review how effectively they engaged the conflict and each other.

We place the name of this tool in quotes to indicate that we don't necessarily intend for teams to take the suggestion literally. That said, when teams have the opportunity to videotape team meetings, we absolutely endorse the idea. We often use videotaping in our work with teams. We find that team members are sometimes astounded by what they see and hear on tape. At the same time, we recognize the impractical nature of videotaping every team interaction. Use it when you can. Otherwise do your best to employ some of the same concepts without the tape.

After a team has wrestled with a conflict, they can schedule a specific time to discuss and debrief the conflict. The idea is to reposition the discussion from "inside the conflict" to "outside the conflict." When done well, they essentially "review the tape" of their recent conflict, analyzing behaviors and processes that had negative and positive impacts on the conflict. In other words, the technique requires team members to discuss the conflict as if they were discussing a movie they had all recently seen.

This technique is especially meaningful to me (Tim) because my family loves movies. We have our favorites, of course. *The Lord of the Rings* series is among our most cherished. My wife (Mac) and both children (Lindsay and Kyle) have also read all the related books by J.R.R. Tolkien. I think I read *The Hobbit* once a very long time ago. It's also important to note that I have a particular penchant for "not getting" critical elements of most of the movies I've ever seen. Although this makes watching the same movies over and over again quite entertaining, it also leads to some engaging discussions with my family.

I apologize to those of you who have not seen the *Lord of the Rings* movies or read the books. The level of detail in the stories is extensive. The example that follows therefore may not contain quite the level of intended impact for those unfamiliar with Tolkien's work. For the example here, I'll give just a smidgen of detail to enhance your understanding. In this abbreviated description, I certainly have not done justice to the storyline; nevertheless, I'm fairly confident that the example of my family's discussion about the movie illustrates the value of reviewing the tape.

In the case of *The Lord of the Rings*, I had a rather difficult time with the character Gollum. In addition to finding his dialogue hard to understand, I just didn't get the significance of his role. Why was this little, creepy, part-human, part-hobbit, part-animal sort of creature talking to himself all the time? And why was he so interested in the ring? I didn't fully share my disdain for Gollum with Mac, Lindsay, or Kyle until I had seen the movies several times. They explained to me that Gollum had transformed into his current state after having existed earlier in life as Smeagol. Smeagol had originally been a hobbit-like creature who had murdered a friend during an argument over the precious ring. His existence as Gollum was the result of a curse placed on him due to his murderous ways. My wife and kids even forwarded the DVD to the scene showing the argument so I could see for myself. Imagine my surprise as I exclaimed, "Oh, now it makes sense!" much to the amusement of my family. The misunderstanding was resolved, and I have a new-found fascination with Gollum, even though I still don't like him very much. Mac, Lindsay, Kyle, and I are finally on the same wavelength (or at least closer) about the movies and the characters. Reviewing the movie with my family has expanded my appreciation and understanding, and my reputation for bungling important information has been preserved!

When team members can have a discussion about themselves in a similar way, they may find that their perceptions of certain parts of recent interactions are not aligned. They may discover that the way one team member remembers a discussion may be different from the way others recall it. The impact of every action on each team member may be slightly, if not immensely, different for each member. When such differences in impact are not recognized in the moment, perceptions quickly become facts, and reactions can become destructive.

The technique of discussing the recent conflict as observers of it rather than participants in it reduces the risk that emotions will flare and interfere with the analysis. It is yet another way to maximize focus on the task conflict while soothing the potential for relationship conflict. An examination of the situation as third parties allows a more objective perspective of the conflict. Reviewing the tape can assist team members in preventing misunderstandings, misperceptions, and miscommunications from becoming the facts on which they base their relationships and trust in one another. This tool helps teams process their behaviors and interactions so they can reap the value from their differences and disagreements rather than suffer the pain of assumed poor intent.

## Conclusion

All teams will find themselves engaged in conflict at some point. We hope that not all conflicts will be perceived negatively. Rather, conflict will be seen as a sign of healthy diversity among team members. As a team's competence in engaging conflict grows, diversity of views manifests into wider ranges of potential solutions to challenges. The team leverages conflict constructively and reduces the harmful effects on its climate.

The techniques described in this chapter are not panaceas, and the list of techniques provided is not exhaustive. Most important, techniques alone cannot replace a climate of trust, true respect for teammates, and genuine, mindful communication among team members. Techniques, however, can provide assistance for confronting conflict affirmatively rather than falling victim to it. Team members, team leaders, and team facilitators can use these techniques to explore conflicts confidently. Whenever conflicts begin to take a toll, these techniques can help team members regain control, refocus their energy, and understand how they "behaved" themselves into the conflict in the first place.

In the next chapter, we examine some special circumstances that teams may face. The potential difficulties presented by distance, diversity, and the use of technology for communication can make team conflicts even more challenging.

# 6

# SPECIAL CASES: VIRTUAL
# AND GLOBAL TEAMS

We don't see things as they are; we see things as we are.

—*Anaïs Nin*

Changes in the global business environment, technology, and organizational structures have created new and challenging environments for teams. These challenges include learning how to deal with conflict in a variety of circumstances. Here, we examine two types of teams that have become increasingly prevalent and encounter a number of special conflict issues: virtual teams and global teams.

Virtual teams, which are sometimes also called distributed teams or e-teams, have members who are separated by distance and have to rely on technology for their communications (Zaccaro and Bader, 2003). Global teams, also referred to as multicultural teams, consist of members from different cultural backgrounds. These cultures have characteristic ways of thinking and responding to issues that are shared among members of the group but often differ from other cultures (Gibson and Manuel, 2003). Frequently teams contain both virtual and multicultural elements. Global teams, out of necessity, communicate through technological means. Many virtual and traditional teams have growing diversity, drawing members from different cultural backgrounds.

Virtual and global teams have many things in common with traditional teams: they need to work together to accomplish common goals, have to be able to get the best out of diversity, and avoid the downsides of relationship conflict. They face unique challenges with respect to conflict because of their structure, makeup, and communication processes.

In this chapter, we examine some of the unique sources of conflict for both virtual and global teams. We also look at the challenges that conflict presents for these teams and discuss ways in which virtual and global teams can address these challenges.

## The Challenges of Being Virtual

Conflict in virtual teams derives from many of the same sources as conflict found in traditional teams whose members work in the same location: people see things differently. When these differences are perceived to be incompatible or threatening, they can result in destructive conflict.

Members of virtual teams usually see each other less frequently than traditional team members do. Some of their frustrations and conflict emerge from not knowing each other well enough. This lack of familiarity creates a lack of trust, which can exacerbate conflict. Communications can be more difficult in virtual teams. Lag times between sending messages and receiving responses are almost always slower than in face-to-face contexts, making it difficult to develop mutual understanding of issues (Cramton, 2001). This can also impede the creation of team ground rules. Lack of familiarity, coupled with difficulty in communicating and understanding, can also lead to misattributions, which are often at the heart of relationship conflict (Cramton, 2002).

The virtual team environment presents a number of challenges for team leaders and team members in being able to recognize and respond to conflict effectively. In virtual teams, communications take place through technology, which can make understanding more difficult. Without the ability to read body language and facial expressions, it is harder to recognize when someone is upset about an issue. Typically conflict unfolds more gradually in virtual teams because communications are slower and conflict takes longer to build. This often makes it difficult to recognize when conflict is present (Armstrong and Cole, 2002). Without visual cues, it is difficult to interpret the meaning of silence. Are people upset and avoiding the conflict, or are they fine and just have nothing to say? Leaders of virtual teams must stay more alert for the presence of conflict. If they suspect that conflict may be present, they should check with their colleagues to see if it is.

Even when information is shared, distributed teams have more difficulty developing a common understanding or meaning about data and information. When team members work in different contextual settings, they may not understand one another based on words. If one team member is trying to describe a particular approach to fixing a part on an engine and a teammate in another location is working on a different version of the same engine, they may be using similar terms that have different meanings. The process is complicated by lag times associated with asynchronous forms of communications: e-mail and other types of communications in which interactions do not take place in real time (Kankanhalli, Tan, and Wei, 2007). These communication difficulties and information-sharing problems also lead to identity issues. Members of distributed teams often have a problem thinking of themselves as a team when they cannot see and interact on a regular basis with their colleagues (Mortensen and Hinds, 2001).

## Emotional Intelligence

Technology-mediated communication can sometimes exacerbate tension in teams. People tend to say things in an e-mail that they never would say in person. It seems they feel less inhibited than in face-to-face contexts. Unrestrained responses often lead to hurtful comments shared not only with the intended recipient but also with the entire team. At other times, technology tends to filter out tensions. It buffers the degree to which people recognize tensions. People may choose not to respond and let the conflict simmer.

As a consequence, leaders need to be on the lookout for signs of stress among team members. They may need to check in with individual team members more frequently.

Some of the effects of technology are dependent on the technology that is used. In some instances, e-mail may prove helpful in dealing with conflicts. Usually more robust technologies that enable audio, video, and other communication functions will be more effective in managing conflict in virtual teams (Duarte and Snyder, 2006). When tensions are running high, face-to-face meetings may be required.

## Constructive Communications

Communications in virtual teams are often slower than in traditional teams. Slower response times and tendencies to avoid conflict can make constructive communications more difficult. Even the amount of communication can complicate the process in virtual teams. When e-mail constitutes the primary medium of exchange, heavy volume can overwhelm team members (Kankanhalli, Tan, and Wei, 2007). Since it is difficult to develop shared meaning because of communication lags, differences in contextual settings, and the complex nature of group communications, constructive communication represents a major challenge for virtual teams.

## Addressing the Challenges

Perceptions can be very important in virtual teams. Members initially lack familiarity with and trust in one another, so leaders should consider convening an early face-to-face team meeting (Katzenbach and Smith, 2001). This presents an opportunity for the team members to share personal information and get to know one another better. An early meeting also enables the team to begin to build a sense of trust and safety, which is of critical importance for effective functioning and conflict management in virtual teams (Lipnack and Stamps, 1997). The leader may schedule team-building exercises to help with this process.

Team members should work on creating shared understanding about the team's goals and requirements, as well as about individual roles and responsibilities. Since they see each other less frequently than traditional team members do, it is particularly important that they have a mutual understanding of their goal and their individual contributions to reaching it. It is more difficult to clarify confusion in virtual teams, so getting things right at the start takes on special importance in preventing future conflicts. Part of this includes recognizing each other's workplace context to uncover differences in settings that could create communication difficulties (Hinds and Bailey, 2003).

The team can use an initial meeting to begin creating team norms related to communications and conflict. As we saw in traditional teams, creating process norms is essential for avoiding problems down the line. In virtual teams, setting ground rules early is even more important (Griffith, Mannix, and Neale, 2003). Virtual teams require more detailed and explicit standards than traditional teams because they have more complicated communication patterns. Standards should include guidelines for when to use e-mail, telephone, or other technologies. They should also deal with patterns and timing of communications, including how soon to respond to messages (Montoya-Weiss, Mersey, and Sony, 2001).

Norms that support building and maintaining trust and safety are crucial for dealing effectively with conflict. As in the case with traditional teams, leaders need to encourage team members not to talk behind each other's backs or take advantage of one another. They should encourage openness and monitor psychological safety within the team. They should display respect to others on the team and carefully listen to team members (Center for Creative Leadership, 2006a).

The norms need to support constructive communications behaviors such as listening for understanding and perspective taking. They should also incorporate clear methods for how the team will address conflicts when they arise that will emphasize benefiting from different perspectives and refraining from behaviors that are known to induce relationship conflict (Gibson and Manuel, 2003).

After the team has developed familiarity, trust, shared understanding of goals and roles, and norms for effective communications and conflict management, the leader needs to remain alert to any conflict and deal with it constructively. By checking in with individual team members and reviewing team communications, the leader can sense when conflict is happening.

At times the leader will want to stimulate debate while reminding everyone about the norms for keeping task conflict constructive. The leader should encourage members to share their thoughts on subjects and respectfully listen to others. If task conflict begins to change into relationship conflict, the leader needs to intervene and use communications techniques like videoconferencing or even face-to-face meetings where people can pick up on visual and voice cues about how others are responding. If there are breaches of trust or breakdowns in communication or conflict management norms, the leader again should step in quickly to make sure the issues are addressed quickly.

An example will show how this plays out. The prospect of a major sale to a new client was tantalizing. The company's president found out about the opportunity on an airplane flight, and when she returned, she immediately called her general sales manager (GM). She asked him to put together a team to develop a proposal to implement the new hardware and software needed for the prospect's security system upgrade. The GM set to work bringing together the cross-functional team needed to develop the proposal and eventually implement the project. The finance person was located at headquarters and would be easy to reach. The GM needed his local sales rep to work with the client on the details of the proposal. There were also the production managers in charge of hardware and software development who were in a distant city. They didn't get along very well but were otherwise dependable. Finally, he'd need the managers of the installation and customer support groups. They were located in a third city in two separate offices.

The GM sent out an e-mail to the group asking them to participate in a conference call the next morning about this important new effort. One person couldn't join at the originally scheduled time, but everyone was finally able to agree on a call in the afternoon. Before the call took place, there was already some resentment about why the GM had been put in charge of this project. It was fine to let him work on the sale, but he didn't have the experience to run such a project.

The teleconference, which took place on time, mostly consisted of the GM laying out what he saw needed to be done and how he thought various roles and responsibilities should be divided. Not much discussion took place during the call, but afterward, there was considerable grumbling. Of course, the GM wasn't aware of it because no one talked directly to him. Others were talking, though. In fact, two members of the team complained to the president about how the issue was being handled. When the president talked to him about the issue, the GM got angry. Why hadn't the team members raised the issue in the meeting? After he returned to his office, he sent out a curt e-mail asking team members to talk with him if they had problems. The production manager fired back with an e-mail of his own, complaining that the GM never listened to anyone else. Of course, this e-mail was copied to all the other team members. From there, the situation went downhill, and it took a lot of time and effort to clear the air—time and effort that should have been spent developing the proposal.

There were alternatives that could have provided a better start. The president and GM could have agreed on team members. The initial message outlining the opportunity to the team could have come from the president, who could have mentioned her request to the GM to lead the team effort. The initial meeting could have been face-to-face. The GM could have spent a lot more time listening than talking at first. Although it was necessary to describe the opportunity as they understood it at that point, it was just as important to talk about how they wanted to work together as a team. This would have included how and when they would use different technologies to communicate, how they wanted to address conflicts that arose, and how they wanted to share information and communicate with one another so they could take advantage of the team members' unique experience and skills. Although it is tempting to jump into the substance of what the team would be doing, it is a temptation worth resisting. Getting clear on how the team wants to work with each other is an essential element of being able to address conflict effectively in traditional, and perhaps even more so in virtual, teams.

The norms that team members and leaders use will be affected by the makeup of the team. When team members come from different cultures, both the types of things that cause conflict and acceptable means of managing it change. In the next section we investigate how cultural differences can complicate conflict management in teams.

## Different Cultures, Different Conflicts

Software teams operate twenty-fours hours a day working with team members dispersed around the globe, and customer service frequently functions using global teams. In an era of globalization, it should be no surprise that teams now are frequently made up of members from a variety of cultures. These teams face conflict like all others, but they also have to deal with unique challenges. In this section, we look at different sources of conflict for global teams, the challenges that conflict brings, and approaches these teams can use to address it.

### Sources of Conflict

People from a particular culture share a system of meaning (Ting-Toomey and Takai, 2006). When teams are made up of people from different cultures, they lack this common system and have difficulty understanding one another even when they speak the same language. Misunderstandings can lead to frustration when expectations about how others should act are not met. The uncertainty of how others will act can also create a sense of anxiety among team members, which can make it more difficult to be open with one another.

There are numerous ways in which different cultures believe people should interact with one another. One example involves differences between cultures that put an emphasis on the individual and those that focus more on the collective importance of a community or a team (Ford, 2001). Cultures that put primacy on the individual emphasize individual rewards and recognition. In collectivist cultures, the focus is placed on team rewards and recognition.

Another type of difference involves attitudes about hierarchy. In some cultures, great importance is placed on the position of superiors and subordinates, with deference being given to the opinions of superiors. While this may be true to some extent in most cultures, some prefer a more egalitarian approach that deemphasizes the power difference among members of the team (Gibson and Manuel, 2003). People in Asian, Middle Eastern, and African countries are more accustomed to larger power differences, whereas northern Europe and North American cultures prefer smaller power differences. Each culture adapts its approach to these issues in ways that work for its members. When people from different cultures come together, these differences can cause problems because team members may not understand or agree with the approaches found in the other culture. Members of a team may not immediately recognize this source of frustration, but to be effective, they will need to explore and discuss it.

As in virtual teams, members of global or multicultural teams are usually located in distant settings. They often have to depend on computer-mediated communication, with all of the challenges that those technologies present. So in addition to cultural issues, communication challenges based on technology are present for most global teams. On top of this, team members typically operate in different time zones, so determining effective methods for overcoming temporal differences during communication becomes important. If one set of team members always has to be the one to have late-night telephone calls while others do so during normal working hours, this can present problems.

Other situations can trigger conflict in multicultural teams. If members of the dominant culture within the team expect members of other cultures to assimilate or accommodate to the main culture, tensions can arise. If members of different groups criticize or insult those of another culture or treat them in ways that are perceived to be unfair, conflicts will arise (Center for Creative Leadership, 2006b).

## Challenges

Trying to understand one another is the major challenge for global teams. Language differences present difficulties. In addition, cultural differences affect how people understand the words that are being communicated, particularly when dealing with conflict. When people are experiencing heightened emotions around conflict, communicating effectively can be difficult, even when everyone speaks the same language and has the same cultural background. It is even more difficult for teams whose members speak different languages.

Team members whose native language is different from the common language the team uses will have special difficulty finding the right words to use to describe emotions they are experiencing during conflict (Von Glinow, Shapiro, and Brett, 2004). They may remain quiet, and others may misconstrue this silence as agreement. Members of cultures whose native language is used in the team may take up most of the airtime during discussions, so team leaders must make a special effort to see that all team members are heard.

Members of different cultures have their own unique ways of contextualizing concepts. In individualist cultures, communication tends to be more explicit. The messages themselves describe the intentions of the speaker. In collectivist cultures, communication is more implicit, relying on shared conventions or contexts to provide meaning to the sentiment being expressed (Gibson and Manuel, 2003). Those who do not understand these conventions or contexts will not fully understand the meaning of what is being conveyed.

An even more fundamental difference among cultures is whether it is appropriate to directly talk about conflict. In North America, northern Europe, and Australia, there is a preference for being direct when communicating about conflict. It is summed up by the phrase, "Let's put our cards on the table."

In other cultures, this is not necessarily the case. In Asia and the Middle East, people prefer indirect approaches to discussing conflict; for example, messages might be conveyed through a third party (Hammer, 2005). Talking directly about conflict in teams will be effective only when the participants believe that it is effective and agree to participate in that manner.

Earlier we mentioned that conflict can produce anxiety when we deal with people from different cultures. We do not know how our colleagues from different cultures will respond, and this creates uncertainty. This anxiety can lead to people preferring to avoid conflict rather than dealing with it. Since global team members who are geographically dispersed rarely see one another, it becomes easier for them to avoid it. In these cases, conflict may simmer and create problems down the line.

When there are several members of each culture on a team, it is natural that they will be more comfortable with others from their own culture, and subgroups can form within the team. These subgroups can reinforce negative, stereotypical attributions of other subgroups, which can lead to relationship conflict. These categorical attributions may not be easy to observe, though, particularly when they are discussed only within the subgroups (Kankanhalli, Tan, and Wei, 2007).

## Addressing the Challenges

Global or multicultural teams need to do many of the same kinds of preparation as virtual teams to address conflict. We recommend that they specifically address processes and procedures for handling conflict and communications at the outset. As with virtual teams, a face-to-face meeting may be particularly helpful in setting the right tone.

Global teams can benefit from cultural training (Dubé and Paré, 2001). In addition to general exploration of cultural differences, such training can identify and examine potential sources of conflict for the team related to cultural differences. It can verify types of cultural diversities found in the team and foster discussion about how these may lead to conflict. It can also help team members discover how different cultures prefer to address conflict when it occurs (Kankanhalli, Tan, and Wei, 2007).

Understanding the needs of team members from different cultures is important to enable them to be able to work together well, so they can make the best out of their diversity and keep conflicts from derailing their collaborative efforts. Our colleague Michael Rawlings, an expert in facilitation, coaching, and mediation, uses a particularly effective technique when he asks team members two key questions at the outset. The first question is, "What will it take for you to bring yourself fully to the team process?" This is a positive way of exploring the needs of team members that, if met, can ensure active collaboration in the team. The second question is, "What has not worked well for you with past teams, and how can we address the problem at the start this time?" This question looks for issues that are difficult for team members and allows them to be surfaced and addressed early.

## Communication Norms

Developing norms for communications before and during conflict is an important task for global teams. The time to do this is early on, before conflict emerges (Gibson and Manuel, 2003).

The communication norms should address how and when communications take place and coordinate their timing when members live in different time zones (Montoya-Weiss, Mersey, and Sony, 2001). They also need to address the technologies that will be used for different types of communications.

In general, the communication norms must address the roles, responsibilities, and expectations of team members regarding communications and provide a way for teammates to communicate constructively and supportively. There needs to be a sense of predictability and consistency about the process (Bandow, 2001).

In order to prevent communications difficulties from becoming the source of team conflict, teams should develop a clear approach for managing communications. One element is to check with each other to make sure that there is shared understanding of important points. Another norm can encourage team members not to interrupt others while they are speaking because this type of self-control can prevent destructive conflict. Finally, if communications do begin to sour, the team needs to have an agreed-on method for cooling things down and getting itself back on the right track (Ayoko, Härtel, and Callan, 2002). It may be necessary for the team to employ a facilitator to help with these difficult challenges, particularly when cultural differences make communications problematic (Paul, Samarah, Seetharaman, and Mykytyn, 2004).

The team should address how it wants to respond when conflicts occur. In some cases, conflict is desirable, but as we have seen, it is not easy to keep it constructive. The team members need to talk about how they want to debate issues and how they want to address situations where task-focused debate has begun to change into relationship conflict. They can talk about the use of constructive communication behaviors described in Chapter Four, including reflective thinking and delay responding, listening for understanding, perspective taking and empathy, and expressing emotions. This can also include discussion of elements required in creating the right climate, such as the development of trust and safety, behavioral integration, and emotional intelligence.

## Dealing with Emotions

As in the case of traditional teams, dealing with emotions associated with conflict in global teams is critically important. Although people from different cultures may experience different emotions in similar settings, they almost always experience some emotions related to conflict. These may include anger, frustration, or fear.

Once again, mindfulness and reflection can play a key role in controlling one's own emotions, as well as being able to deal effectively with those of others. These processes can relieve anxiety and help us look at others' behaviors in new ways. By being aware of our own cultural assumptions, we can become open to looking at different perspectives not as wrong but as different. We can observe conflict less judgmentally and keep from getting caught up in negative emotions and thoughts just because someone acts differently than we think they should. This allows us not only to be concerned with our own interests but to care about other people's need to save face, and it can result in better handling of conflict. "The more members of a culturally diverse group who have other- or mutual-face concerns in the forefront, the more likely the multicultural team will engage in effective conflict communication management and outcome" (Ting-Toomey and Takai, 2006, p. 717).

## The Role of the Leader

Team leaders need to show the way by personal example. Their behaviors, attitudes, and styles can influence outcomes in both virtual and global teams. Being open to hearing a variety of perspectives can help build trust in teams and lead to effective conflict resolution. Leaders who develop and demonstrate emotional intelligence can encourage their teammates to keep their composure and approach conflict with a task-oriented, problem-solving style (Rahim and Psenicka, 2002).

The leader needs to foster development of team communication and conflict management norms. A clear, early focus on team process can prevent misunderstandings from becoming disagreements and help conflicts stay constructive. The approach may differ based on the makeup of the team (Bandow, 2001). Although the norms and associated behaviors will have common elements, the leader will have to adjust the approaches the team uses to deal with conflict based on the cultural background of its members. Sometimes more direct discussion of the issues will be called for, and in other cases, a more indirect, behind-the-scenes approach may be necessary. This will require the leader to learn more about the cultural approaches to conflict represented by the members of the team.

## In Practice

A team leader in a Fortune Global 100 company contacted our colleague Maya Hu-Chan for help with conflict issues that were affecting the team's performance. Maya is an international management consultant specializing in global leadership and cross-cultural training, and the team was made up of members from Korea, China, Taiwan, Japan, India, and South Africa. The team leader was British and was headquartered in Singapore. The team had been together for one year and was not meeting its goals.

Maya initially interviewed team members and had them take assessment instruments to get a better sense of the team's effectiveness in the areas of leadership, decision making, communications, and conflict management. She wanted to know what areas were critical for team success and which of those were presenting the greatest challenges. After this preparation, it became clear that the team was having considerable difficulties with communication and conflict management.

The team members were having a hard time understanding one other. They all spoke English in varying degrees of proficiency.

The problems arose more from communication styles, though, than from language issues. Some members of the team preferred direct communication styles, while others preferred indirect approaches. Since most of the communications were by e-mail, the people who preferred more direct communications tended to send most of the messages. Sometimes members for whom English was a second language also communicated less often. These patterns were leading to some resentment and distrust. Over time people began communicating less and less. Trust suffered, and team members stopped sharing information and working collaboratively.

Maya encouraged the team leader to call a face-to-face meeting of the team, which subsequently took place in Singapore. On the first day of the session, Maya presented some of the results from her initial interviews and the assessments. She then encouraged team members to voice concerns and recommended a norm of open sharing in the workshop. The team members wanted to achieve better results, so in spite of some initial reluctance, they began sharing concerns about their communications processes.

The first evening the team went to a local restaurant that served classic Singaporean cuisine. The team members were able to loosen up and get to know one another on a more personal basis, something they had not done when the team was formed. Maya noticed that the sessions went much better on the second day because people were more comfortable with each other and more willing to talk openly.

The team took the concerns from the first day and began developing norms for how they wanted to handle communications going forward. These ground rules included a number of do's and don'ts for interacting with one another, such as don't make assumptions, understand each other's circumstances, show respect during communication, and do not start communications with a negative attitude (they described this with the phrase, "No, but . . .").

The team left the meeting with a new level of understanding and trust in one another and a new set of norms to help guide their communications processes. Maya received a note from the team leader later in the year indicating that the ground rules were being followed and that the team was communicating better and working collaboratively to address conflicts. More than that, the team's production was up over 50 percent from prior levels.

A team does not have to wait until it is in trouble to address these issues. Michael Rawlings told us about a team in an international financial institution that dealt with them at the beginning. Michael was called in to facilitate a strategic planning session between a multicultural group in the institution's home office and an information technology (IT) outsourcing group in India. They needed to develop a plan for providing customer support for IT functions. The group was not able to meet in person because of travel restrictions, so the sessions were going to be conducted by videoconference.

Michael had substantial experience working with global teams and knew that cultural differences and communication challenges could lead to conflicts that could jeopardize the outcome of the planning work. He spent considerable time talking with the team members in the home office and the staff in India about how they wanted to conduct the sessions. He engaged a facilitator in India to work closely with him in making sure that opinions of people on both ends of the communication were effectively heard.

Michael and the other facilitator worked at managing expectations and uncovering possible pitfalls. They also worked with each group to develop a common set of communication and conflict management norms. In particular, they agreed that if it appeared that misunderstandings were developing or that relationship conflict was starting to emerge, they would pause the proceedings to get things clarified and back on track. By having facilitators on both ends of the videoconference, they were better able to recognize signs of problems earlier and address them before they derailed the proceedings. This all took time, but in the end, the strategic planning sessions were a success, and follow-up implementation went well.

## Next Steps

In Chapters Three through Six, we have looked at various approaches that traditional, virtual, and global teams can use to deal more effectively with conflict: creating the right climate, using constructive communication behaviors and techniques, and adapting to unique challenges posed by distance and culture. In our final chapter, we provide some simple, practical tools that you can use to begin the process of improving your team's ability to address conflict.

# 7

# GETTING STARTED ON THE ROAD TO CONFLICT COMPETENCE

> Difference of opinion leads to enquiry, and enquiry to truth.
>
> —*Thomas Jefferson*

In our experience, most teams that seek assistance for dealing with conflict have not spent enough time discussing and agreeing on process issues. We hope you've talked with your teammates about conflict—how you've handled it in the past, and how you plan to handle it in the future. We know, however, that conflict isn't always the easiest topic to engage, so we have a few simple suggestions that can provide some structure as you and your teammates begin.

We thought it would be useful to supply you with a series of tools to help you and your teammates take some first steps in assessing your conflict competence and addressing improvement opportunities. This chapter has been specifically designed with utility in mind. Despite what librarians, teachers, and parents taught you about never writing in books, we encourage you to fill up the following pages! And feel free to make copies of these tools for use with your team.

Most teams already have a general sense of how effectively they're addressing conflict. In other words, they are adept at monitoring their team temperature. Teams generally know when things are going great, and they know when they've hit a challenge. A general sense, however, may not be enough to spur a team to action. Furthermore, teammates probably have different and unique perspectives about the team's conflict competence.

It is critical that these differences are acknowledged and shared for the team to truly make progress. Thus, we've created the tools in this chapter. We encourage you and your teammates to use them to assess where you are, determine what areas deserve the most attention, and ultimately decide how to begin building more competence and confidence in the areas of most need.

We have created five tools for your consideration and use. First, we offer a series of questions that are useful in assessing individual team members' readiness to address conflict. These questions help you and your teammates anticipate potential sources of conflict and assess your personal effectiveness in handling conflict when it occurs. Next, we present a similar worksheet that is helpful in assessing and analyzing the team's readiness for conflict. The focus here is on the team's general approach to conflict. Third, we suggest a brief evaluation of several foundational issues: goals, roles, values, and norms. As teams reflect on these points, they readily identify opportunities for continued development. The fourth tool helps you consider five essential components for creating the right climate for conflict competence on your team. Here you can evaluate five specific aspects of your current team climate. Finally, we have created assessments for examining your team's competence in the four constructive behaviors and skills necessary for building and maintaining conflict competent teams. These assessments enable you to apply the same evaluation method used for analyzing your team climate to the quality of your team's communication.

At the conclusion of each segment, we offer some suggestions for building on strengths and addressing development opportunities. These suggestions can and should be tailored to fit your team's unique characteristics and situation.

Contained in this chapter are:

- Team Member Readiness Questions
- Team Readiness Questions
- Team Foundations Worksheet
- Assessing Your Team Climate
- Assessing Your Team's Communication

## Team Member Readiness Questions

These questions can be used in several ways. One option is to have team members individually review the questions. They write out answers in advance and then meet together to share their perspectives. A second option is to conduct an open team discussion using the questions as a guide. We recommend that the team document the discussions for review and more analysis in the future. A third option is to address one or two questions during each team meeting over a period of time. Again, we recommend the use of documentation to ensure that valuable communication points are not lost. Finally, we suggest that these questions can be used repeatedly by teams over time to reassess and renew their commitment to addressing conflict effectively. We encourage you and your team to find your own best practices in using these questions, and to share your methods with other teams.

1. How would you describe your personal approach to addressing conflict?

2. What do you do best when it comes to addressing conflict?

3. Where can you most improve when handling conflict?

4. Are your conflicts mostly task conflicts, relationship conflicts, or a combination of the two? Provide some examples.

5. What two things could you do to improve your overall conflict competence?

## Analysis and Suggestions

• *Questions 1–3:* As team members share their responses to these questions, listen and look at patterns and trends. This will help you determine whether team members share similar conceptual views and have similar approaches for engaging conflict. For instance, if most team members describe their approach to conflict as avoiding, the team might want to consider establishing agreements that encourage the thorough examination of all conflicting views. If most team members report that what they do best when addressing conflict is convincing others to see it their way, you may decide to explore ways for ensuring consistent perspective taking when discussing opposing ideas.

• *Question 4:* In general, when your teammates perceive that their conflicts are more task related than relationship related, the more likely you'll find that your team is able to engage in vigorous debates effectively. If most of your teammates report that their conflicts are relationship oriented, it may be wise to spend time reviewing Chapter Four to brush up on constructive conflict skills and behaviors.

• *Question 5:* We suggest creating a comprehensive list as team members share their responses to this question. This list alone can help the team decide what steps to take for improving their climate, skills, and behaviors.

Finally, a powerful way to assess the individual conflict competence of team members is to use an assessment tool such as the Conflict Dynamics Profile (CDP). Check the Resources section at the end of the book to learn more about this instrument.

## Team Readiness Questions

Like the team member readiness questions, this worksheet can be completed individually and then reviewed in a team meeting or used for a guided discussion among team members. The worksheet first provides general discussion questions and then focuses on four key areas that provide a solid foundation for team development and conflict competence:

1. How would you describe your team's general approach to addressing conflict?

2. What topics are the most likely to foster conflicting views among team members?

3. Are your team conflicts mostly task conflicts, relationship conflicts, or a combination of the two? Provide some examples.

4. What does the team do best when it comes to addressing conflict?

5. Where can the team most improve when handling conflict?

6. What do other members of the organization, clients, customers, and vendors perceive about the team's conflict competence?

7. What two things could you do to improve the team's overall conflict competence?

## Analysis and Suggestions

As in the team member readiness section, we encourage you and your teammates to analyze the responses to each of the open-ended questions independently. Questions 1, 3, 4, 5, and 7 are very similar to the questions asked of individuals. We suggest that you share, discuss, and analyze these questions in much the same way:

• *Question 2:* Responses to this question can help your team become more proactive. Many team members anticipate topics that challenge the team. This question enables team members to move beyond anticipation. Once the list is created and published, anticipation turns to action. It's similar to planning a trip. When we know where the highway is under construction, we can make choices regarding route. We encourage teams to plan their routes so potential conflicts or roadblocks can be handled more effectively.

• *Question 6:* This question first asks team members to share perceptions. Once the perceptions are clear, team members may wish to verify those perceptions by asking their constituents for feedback. We believe that the consistent seeking of feedback from those who work with the team is an effective way for the team to stay aware of its impact on others.

## Team Foundations Worksheet

In this section, use a ten-point scale to evaluate your team's readiness regarding goals, roles, values, and norms. Once again, we recommend that teammates complete this worksheet independently first, then share results during a team meeting.

| Always/Completely | | Usually | Sometimes | | Rarely | | Never/Not at All | |
|---|---|---|---|---|---|---|---|---|
| 10 | 9 | 8 | 7 | 6 | 5 | 4 | 3 | 2 | 1 |

### Team Goals

\_\_\_\_Our team goals are clear and understood by all team members.

\_\_\_\_My team reviews and discusses progress toward our goals.

\_\_\_\_My team celebrates when we achieve or exceed our goals.

\_\_\_\_My team conducts a thorough review when we miss our targets.

### Team Roles

\_\_\_\_My teammates and I have clearly defined roles and responsibilities.

\_\_\_\_We all know and understand one another's roles and responsibilities.

\_\_\_\_When roles change, we clarify how the changes affect the team.

\_\_\_\_The role of team leadership is clear and understood by all team members.

### Team Values

\_\_\_\_We take time to identify and discuss our team values.

\_\_\_\_We share team values and consistently support them.

\_\_\_\_When team values are violated, we address the situation.

\_\_\_\_We demonstrate our team values in all team interactions.

## Team Norms

____Team members know and support our team norms and agreements.

____Our team's success is based on our commitment to our team agreements.

____New norms evolve and are easily adjusted whenever conditions change.

____Team members behave consistently in accordance with our agreements.

## Analysis and Suggestions

A general method for evaluating the responses is for each team member to provide a total number of points assigned to each of the four categories. The team can easily determine the average score for each category. Chapter Three is a good resource for teams that need to take action in any of the four areas assessed. We suggest the following guidelines when analyzing the team averages:

32–40  Congratulations! The team is performing well. Corrective action is not necessary.

24–31  Good! There is some room for growth, however. Review current views and agreements, and adjust where necessary.

12–23  Caution! Improvement is needed. The team should begin a thorough assessment of this category and seek guidance or assistance for improvement.

0–11  Warning! The team is not functioning well. This area requires immediate attention.

## Assessing Your Team Climate: Components for Establishing the Right Climate

Five essential components for establishing the right climate are considered in the questions below. Use the following scale to indicate your level of agreement with each item. Give each item a rating or numerical score. Next, add the items to arrive at a total score for each component.

**Scale:**

4   I agree.

3   I agree more than I disagree.

2   I disagree more than I agree.

1   I disagree.

### Attitudes

_____Most team members approach conflict as an opportunity rather than an obstacle.

_____Most team members have had experience dealing with difficult conflicts in the past.

_____As a general rule, nobody on the team fears or avoids conflict.

_____We have shared our perspectives and views about conflict.

_____My teammates would agree that differences should be embraced, not eliminated.

_____**Attitudes total**

### Trust

_____I believe that my teammates have my best interests at heart.

_____My teammates are skilled and capable of producing excellent results.

_____My teammates share the same basic values.

_____Our team leader is trustworthy.

_____I believe that my teammates have integrity and communicate with me honestly.

_____**Trust total**

## Safety

_____Team members show genuine empathy and concern for one another.

_____I am willing to take risks and be vulnerable with my teammates.

_____Team members are willing to disagree even when in the minority.

_____Team members are never taken advantage of by others on the team.

_____Team members have a strong sense of mutual respect.

_____**Safety total**

## Working Together (Behavioral Integration)

_____My teammates share information freely and frequently.

_____Team members readily give each other the benefit of the doubt when sharing views.

_____Teammates explore issues deeply and engage in vigorous debate.

_____Team members are interdependent and rely on each other heavily.

_____Individual team members identify themselves as members of this team to others.

_____**Working Together total**

## Emotional Intelligence

_____My teammates recognize that internal conflicts are inevitable and natural.

_____My team has discussed how we will deal with emotional issues.

_____Team members have shared their personal hot buttons with each other.

_____Most team members are adept at displaying empathy with one another.

_____My team knows how to cool down and slow down when things get intense.

_____**Emotional Intelligence total**

## Individual Summary

_____ Attitudes                 _____Trust

_____Safety                      _____Working Together

_____Emotional Intelligence

## Team Total Summary

_____Attitudes                  _____Trust

_____Safety                      _____Working Together

_____Emotional Intelligence

## Team Averages

_____Attitudes                  _____Trust

_____Safety                      _____Working Together

_____Emotional Intelligence

## Analysis and Suggestions

Add all team members' total component scores together to determine a team total for each component. Then divide each team total by the number of team members who completed the checklist. This results in a team average score for each component. The components with the lowest relative averages are most in need of attention for establishing the right team climate.

Chapter Three provides guidance on how to maintain and leverage team strengths or improve in areas of opportunity. Use the following guidelines to assess your team's effectiveness:

*3.5 and higher:* This is a team strength area:

- Actively reinforce teammates who demonstrate effectiveness.
- Consider how this strength can be leveraged in other areas for improvement.
- Celebrate!

*2.9 to 3.4:* This area is solid but could be improved:

- Schedule time during a team meeting to discuss this area.
- Actively reinforce teammates who demonstrate effectiveness.
- Consider use of the Observation technique from Chapter Five.

*2.0 to 2.8:* This area is in definite need of improvement.

- Schedule a single topic team meeting to address this area.
- Refer to Chapter Three for grounding in this area.
- Techniques such as Stop, Start, Continue; Clearing the Air; and Brainstorming may be useful.

*1.9 and lower:* This is cause for real concern:

- Ask all team members to spend time reflecting on this issue.
- Consider the use of an outside expert or facilitator for assistance.
- Prepare for a thorough assessment of the team's climate.

## Assessing Your Team's Communication: An Examination of Behaviors and Skills

Four major communication sets are critical for conflict competent teams. This tool enables you to assess your team's current effectiveness in these areas. Use the following scale as you analyze each question. Give each item a rating or numerical score. Next, add the items to arrive at a total score for each category.

### Scale

4   Excellent or almost always; we perform very well.

3   Good or usually; but we could improve.

2   Average or sometimes; we could definitely benefit by improvement here.

1   Below average or seldom; this is cause for real concern.

### Reflective Thinking and Delay Responding

_____My teammates call for time-outs when discussions become too heated.

_____Our team leader senses when we need a break.

_____Our team temporarily tables decisions when we have significant disagreements.

_____Team members coach each other to cool down, slow down, and reengage.

_____We give each other opportunities to think things over.

_____**Reflective Thinking and Delay Responding total**

### Perspective Taking and Empathy

_____During important discussions, we ask many questions.

_____When differences arise, we explore them fully.

_____My teammates go out of their way to check for understanding.

_____Teammates are good at acknowledging and describing each other's feelings.

_____Our team leader effectively summarizes key points made during meetings.

_____**Perspective Taking and Empathy total**

## Expressing Emotions

_____Team members are honest about their feelings and emotions.

_____My teammates seldom raise their voices, swear, or use accusatory language.

_____When asked by others, teammates admit feelings such as frustration or concern.

_____We routinely engage in straight talk with each other.

_____My teammates share good news and accomplishments freely.

_____**Expressing Emotions total**

## Listening for Understanding

_____Team members leave team meetings with a good sense of where everybody stands.

_____We seldom interrupt or cut one another off.

_____My teammates ask lots of questions when trying to understand other points of view.

_____Team members encourage the use of examples, analogies, and metaphors.

_____On the whole, we are a team of very good listeners.

_____**Listening for Understanding total**

## Individual Summary

\_\_\_\_Reflective Thinking and Delay Responding

\_\_\_\_Perspective Taking and Empathy

\_\_\_\_Expressing Emotions

\_\_\_\_Listening for Understanding

## Team Total Summary

\_\_\_\_Reflective Thinking and Delay Responding

\_\_\_\_Perspective Taking and Empathy

\_\_\_\_Expressing Emotions

\_\_\_\_Listening for Understanding

## Team Averages

\_\_\_\_Reflective Thinking and Delay Responding

\_\_\_\_Perspective Taking and Empathy

\_\_\_\_Expressing Emotions

\_\_\_\_Listening for Understanding

## Analysis and Suggestions

Adding all team members' total component scores together gives a team total for each component. Divide each team total by the number of team members who completed the exercise to get a team average score for each component. The components with the lowest relative averages are most in need of attention for establishing the right team climate.

Chapter Four is a great resource for guidance on maintaining and leveraging team strengths or improving areas of need. Use the following guidelines as you consider your team's results and action steps:

*3.5 and higher:* This is a team strength area:

- Actively reinforce teammates who demonstrate effectiveness.

- Consider how this strength can be leveraged in other areas for improvement.

- Celebrate!

*2.9 to 3.4:* This area is solid but could be improved:

- Schedule time during a team meeting for discussion of this area.

- Use team-building activities and exercises to enhance development in areas for improvement.

- Consider use of the Reviewing the Tape and Reframing Through Inquiry techniques from Chapter Five.

*2.0 to 2.8:* This area is in definite need of improvement:

- Schedule a single topic team meeting to address this area.

- Consider the use of an outside expert or facilitator for assistance.

- Techniques such as Peer Feedback; Stop, Start, Continue; Clearing the Air; and Mediation may be useful.

*1.9 and lower:* This is cause for real concern:

- Ask all team members to commit to improving their skills in this area.
- Consider using individual assessment instruments to identify specific behavioral gaps.
- Use specific training interventions to target team and individual areas for improvement.

## Summary

These few simple assessments are offered as a way to *begin* the exploration of your team's attitudes toward and ability to deal with conflict. But don't limit yourself to just the questions listed here. The key is finding ways to communicate fully and openly about the natural differences and diversity among your teammates. These kinds of conversations can become rich and satisfying dialogues leading to a climate of true collaboration and the development of your team's conflict competence.

# Epilogue

Conflict is the primary engine of creativity and
innovation.

*—Ronald Heifetz*

On August 15, 2003, for one of the very few times since their
historic gold medal performance twenty-three years earlier, the
members of the 1980 U.S. Olympic Hockey Team gathered. This
reunion was of a much more somber nature than ever before.
Their coach, Herb Brooks, had died several days earlier in a car
accident. Team members reflected again on the often chaotic
relationship forged with Coach Brooks so many years earlier.
They shared stories of their trials, conflicts, and challenges. They
smiled when recalling the climate they created, the interactions
they shared, the relationships they built, and the accomplishments they achieved. Once again they were together as a team.
In many ways, they picked up right where they left off. Born
out of conflict and controversy so many years before, the players
stood again as one to pay their final respects to the man who had
led them to international prominence. The challenge now was
not of conflict or competition. It was that of supporting Coach
Brooks's family in this time of loss and supporting one another.
The climate they established nearly a quarter-century before still
existed. They were there for one another, empathizing, caring,
and giving as a team.

Organizations of all types have come to rely on teams to
carry out their business objectives. In our first book, *Becoming a
Conflict Competent Leader*, we focused on the influence leaders

have regarding the recognition, engagement, and resolution of conflicts in the organization. Leaders alone, however, cannot fully meet this challenge. It takes the effort of every one of us in our roles as team members. We each have the power to choose how we respond to the inevitable conflicts that arise among people. These choices collectively make up the kind of climate we create, the nature of the communications in which we engage, and the processes we follow.

At the very core of our beliefs is the notion that conflicts handled constructively can lead to stronger teams, better decisions, innovative solutions, and profitable results. Many people see conflict as a necessary evil. Put several people together, and there's bound to be conflict at some point. Conflict resolution is characterized as a necessary survival skill for navigating the complexity of modern organizations. We don't dispute that conflict resolution skills are critical for success. We agree that they are. We do assert, however, that conflict competence is transformational in its nature. Conflict competent leaders, teams, and team members not only understand how to confront conflict effectively; they encounter conflict as an opportunity to discover more than they knew before. They engage conflict as a signal that something more than what is currently obvious exists in the perceptions, interests, and ideas of our conflict partners. Indeed, conflict becomes a partnership between and among those in conflict so that the issue at hand is examined, expanded, and embraced.

In this book, we have addressed the well-documented negative consequences of team conflict handled poorly. We also have made the case for how teams can prepare for and address conflict in constructive, satisfying ways. Conflict competent teams are characterized by their proficiency in several key areas. First, they spend time and effort in discussing and agreeing on processes that will guide their interactions. Second, they work diligently to create a climate of trust, openness, and support that enables them to safely debate key issues and address critical concerns. Next, they understand the value of interacting effectively with one another.

They choose appropriate words and deeds that demonstrate their commitment to clear, constructive communication. Finally, teams know how to access and use tools to help them overcome the inevitable obstacles that conflict can present.

In an effort to make this book as realistic and engaging as possible, we included many examples of how conflict has played out in teams. We described techniques and tools that teams can use. We addressed some of the special circumstances and challenges presented by distance, diversity, and technology. And we created a series of short, easy-to-use assessments to encourage you and your teammates to address your level of conflict competence. Our message is simple: get started now. Don't wait for conflict to occur before taking steps to address it. Rather, proactively begin to assess your team's readiness for conflict when no conflict is apparent.

Actor James Earl Jones in his role as Terence Mann in the movie *Field of Dreams* suggested to Kevin Costner, playing the role of Ray Kinsella, that people would want to visit the baseball field Kinsella built in the middle of his Iowa corn field. Kinsella, conflicted over whether to keep the baseball field or sell the farm, listened as Mann uttered his stirring advice: "People will come, Ray. People will most definitely come" (Franish and Robinson, 1989). As you consider your team's future, we hope Terence Mann's advice, slightly altered, provides incentive for you and your teammates. Conflict will come. Conflict will most definitely come. Build your team's conflict competence now in preparation for the conflicts that will most definitely come your way. As you do, you'll discover the rewards of your efforts as you minimize the negative consequences of conflict while capitalizing on the vast opportunities it presents.

Good luck. We'll see you down the road.

**The secret to the Internet card trick described in Chapter Four:** The row of cards displayed first consists of all face cards of different suits. You were asked to remember one of the cards. When you scroll down to the second display, your card has been "predicted" and is now absent from the row of cards presented. The fact is that *every* card is different. For instance, the jack of spades has been replaced by the jack of clubs and the queen of diamonds has been replaced by the queen of hearts. Your attention is on only your card, not all the cards. Gotcha!

# Resources

A number of resources can help your team address conflict more effectively. Several of them are described here.

## Leadership Development Institute

We work at the Leadership Development Institute at Eckerd College (LDI), which was founded in 1980 to help individuals and organizations achieve their potential. LDI has been a network associate of the Center for Creative Leadership since 1981 and has delivered internationally acclaimed programs to thousands of corporate, governmental, and nonprofit clients around the world.

LDI offers open enrollment courses, custom programs, and coaching in the fields of leadership, team building, and conflict management. The programs improve participants' awareness of their leadership competencies so they can leverage strengths and develop plans to work on areas of developmental opportunity. LDI has also created the Center for Leadership and Conflict, which develops assessment instruments and programs to improve leaders' skills in dealing with conflict.

Its Conflict Dynamics Profile (CDP) instrument is used by the Center for Creative Leadership and other leadership development organizations to help clients better understand their responses to conflict. The CDP measures people's hot buttons (behaviors in others that tend to upset individuals) as well as the frequency with which they respond with constructive or destructive behaviors when addressing workplace conflict. More information is available about the CDP at www.conflictdynamics.org.

Located in St. Petersburg, Florida, Eckerd College is a private, coeducational college of liberal arts and sciences founded in 1958. Eckerd is a pioneer of responsible innovation—developing programs that have been adopted nationwide and earning the college an international reputation for academic excellence. For more information on LDI, you can call 1–800–753–0444 or visit www.eckerd.edu/ldi.

## Center for Creative Leadership

The Center for Creative Leadership (CCL) is world renowned for its leadership development programs. It also provides training, facilitation, and coaching for teams to help them become more productive. CCL has published a number of materials that deal with team development. These and related publications are listed at http://www.ccl.org/leadership/publications/leadingOthers .aspx?pageId=888. For more information on CCL, you can call 1–336–545–2810 or visit www.ccl.org.

## The Table Group

The Table Group, founded by Patrick Lencioni, provides products, tools, consulting, and speaking services to leaders who want to improve teamwork, clarity, and morale within their companies. Their focus is on helping organizations, and the people who work within them, become healthier and more effective. For more information on the Table Group, you can call 1–925–299–9700 or visit http://www.tablegroup.com.

## Center for Collaborative Organizations

The Center for Collaborative Organizations at the University of North Texas provides knowledge, skills, design and development information, and assistance to build collaborative work systems and enhance teaming. The center hosts annual conferences, public workshops, on-site training, and publications. For more information on the center, you can call 1–940–565–3096 or visit http://www.workteams.unt.edu.

## Interpersonal Communications Programs

Interpersonal Communications Programs (ICP) offers train-the-trainer and on-site instruction in two programs: Collaborative Team Skills for conflict competent team development and the I-SkillsZone for conflict competent leadership development. Both programs are based on concepts and skills originally researched and developed at the University of Minnesota by Sherod Miller and colleagues. The programs teach an integrated system of practical communication skills and processes for collaborative conflict resolution and decision making. Each program provides handy tools for on-the-job training. For more information on ICP, you can call 1–800–328–5099 or visit http://www.i-skillszone.com.

## Mindful Awareness Research Center

The Mindful Awareness Research Center at the Jane and Terry Semel Institute for Neuroscience and Human Behavior at the University of California, Los Angeles, conducts research and provides training in contemplative practices that help in controlling emotions. For more information on the center, you can call 1–310–206–7503 or visit http://www.marc.ucla.edu.

# References

Allred, K. "Anger and Retaliation in Conflict: The Role of Attribution." In M. Deutsch and P. Coleman (eds.), *The Handbook of Conflict Resolution*. San Francisco: Jossey-Bass, 2000.

Amason, A. "Distinguishing the Effects of Functional and Dysfunctional Conflict on Strategic Decision Making: Resolving a Paradox for Top Management Teams." *Academy of Management Journal*, 1996, 39(1), 123–148.

Amason, A., and Sapienza, H. "The Effects of Top Management Team Size and Interaction Norms on Cognitive and Affective Conflict." *Journal of Management*, 1997, 23(4), 495–516.

Amason, A., Thompson, K., Hochwarter, W., and Harrison, A. "Conflict: An Important Dimension in Successful Management Teams." *Organizational Dynamics*, 1995, 24(2), 20–35.

Argyris, C. *Overcoming Organizational Defenses: Facilitating Organizational Learning*. Upper Saddle River, N.J.: Prentice Hall, 1990.

Armstrong, D., and Cole, P. "Managing Distances and Differences in Geographically Distributed Work Groups." In P. Hinds and S. Kiesler (eds.), *Distributed Work*. Cambridge, Mass: MIT Press, 2002.

Ayoko, O., Härtel, C., and Callan, V. "Resolving the Puzzle of Productive and Destructive Conflict in Culturally Heterogeneous Workgroups: A Communication Accommodation Theory Approach." *International Journal of Conflict Management*, 2002, 13(2), 165–195.

Bandow, D. "Time to Create Sound Teamwork." *Journal for Quality and Participation*, Summer 2001, pp. 41–47.

Brefczynski-Lewis, J., and others. "Neural Correlates of Attentional Expertise in Long-Term Meditation Practitioners." *Proceedings of the National Academy of Sciences*, July 3, 2007, pp. 11483–11488.

Capobianco, S., Davis M., and Kraus, L. *Managing Conflict Dynamics: A Practical Approach* (4th ed). St. Petersburg, Fla.: Eckerd College Leadership Development Institute, 2004.

Capobianco, S., Davis M., and Kraus, L. "Good Conflict, Bad Conflict: How to Have One Without the Other." Mt. *Eliza Business Review*, Summer-Autumn 2005, pp. 31–37.

Carmeli, A., and Schaubroeck, J. "Top Management Team Behavioral Integration, Decision Quality, and Organizational Decline." *Leadership Quarterly*, 2006, *17*(5), 441–453.

Center for Creative Leadership. *Leadership Across Differences: Advice to Leaders from Around the World.* Greensboro, N.C.: Center for Creative Leadership, 2006a.

Center for Creative Leadership. *Triggers of Conflicts Related to Differences.* Greensboro, N.C.: Center for Creative Leadership, 2006b.

Chen, M. "Understanding the Benefits and Detriments of Conflict on Team Creative Process." *Creativity and Innovation Management*, 2006, *15*(1), 105–116.

Chowdhery, S. "The Role of Affect- and Cognition-Based Trust in Complex Knowledge Sharing." *Journal of Managerial Issues*, 2005, *17*(3), 310–326.

Coffey, W. *The Boys of Winter: The Untold Story of a Coach, a Dream, and the 1980 U.S. Olympic Hockey Team.* New York: Random House, 2005.

Colvin, G. "Why Dream Teams Fail." *Fortune*, 2006, *153*(11), 87.

Covey, S. *The Seven Habits of Highly Effective People: Powerful Lessons in Personal Change.* New York: Free Press, 1989.

Covey, S., and Merrill, R. *The Speed of Trust: The One Thing That Changes Everything.* New York: Free Press, 2006.

Cramton, C. "The Mutual Knowledge Problem and Its Consequences for Dispersed Collaboration." *Organization Science*, 2001, *12*(3), 346–371.

Cramton, C. "Attribution in Distributed Work Groups." In P. Hinds and S. Kiesler (eds.), *Distributed Work.* Cambridge, Mass.: MIT Press, 2002.

Dana, D. *Managing Differences: How to Build Better Relationships at Work and Home.* (4th ed.) Prairie Mission, Kans.: Dana Mediation Institute, 2005.

Davidson, R., and others. "Alterations in Brain and Immune Function Produced by Mindfulness Meditation." *Psychosomatic Medicine*, 2003, *65*, 564–570.

DeChurch, L., and Marks, M. "Maximizing the Benefits of Task Conflict: The Role of Conflict Management." *International Journal of Conflict Management*, 2001, *12*(1), 4–22.

De Dreu, C. "When Too Little or Too Much Hurts: Evidence for a Curvilinear Relationship Between Task Conflict and Innovation in Teams." *Journal of Management*, 2006, *32*(1), 83–107.

Dooley, R., and Fryxell, G. "Attaining Decision Quality and Commitment from Dissent: The Moderating Effects of Loyalty and Competence in Strategic Decision-Making Teams." *Academy of Management Journal*, 1999, *42*(4), 389–402.

Duarte, D., and Snyder, N. *Mastering Virtual Teams: Strategies, Tools, and Techniques That Succeed.* San Francisco: Jossey-Bass, 2006.

Dubé, L., and Paré, G. "Global Virtual Teams." *Communications of the ACM*, 2001, *44*(12), 71–73.

Dyer, W. G., Dyer, W., Dyer, J., and Schein, E. *Team Building: Proven Strategies for Improving Team Performance.* (4th ed.) San Francisco: Jossey-Bass, 2007.

Edmondson, A. "Psychological Safety, Trust, and Learning in Organizations: A Group-Level Lens." In R. Kramer  and K. Cook  (eds.), *Trust and Distrust in Organizations.* New York: Russell Sage Foundation, 2004.

Edmondson, A., and Smith, D. "Too Hot to Handle? How to Manage Relationship Conflict." *California Management Review*, 2006, 49(1), 6–31.

Eisenhardt, K., Kahwajy, J., and Bourgeois, L. "Conflict and Strategic Choice: How Top Management Teams Disagree." *California Management Review*, 1997a, 39(2), 42–62.

Eisenhardt, K., Kahwajy, J., and Bourgeois, L. "How Management Teams Can Have a Good Fight." *Harvard Business Review*, 1997b, 75(5), 77–85.

Ekman, P. *Emotions Revealed.* New York: Holt, 2003.

Elangovan, A., Werner, A.,  and Szabo, E. "Why Don't I Trust You Now? An Attributional Approach to Erosion of Trust." *Journal of Managerial Psychology*, 2007, *22*(1), 4–24.

Elsbach, K. "Managing Images of Trustworthiness in Organizations." In R. Kramer and K. Cook  (eds.), *Trust and Distrust in Organizations.* New York: Russell Sage Foundation, 2004.

Feyerherm, A., and Rice, C. "Emotional Intelligence and Team Performance: The Good, the Bad and the Ugly." *International Journal of Organizational Analysis*, 2002, *10*(4), 343–362.

Fisher, R., and Shapiro, D. *Beyond Reason.* New York: Viking Press, 2005.

Fisher, R., Ury, W., and Patton, B. *Getting to Yes: Negotiating Agreement Without Giving In.* (2nd ed.) New York: Penguin, 1991.

Flanagan, T. *Last Gasp Gorge.* St. Petersburg, Fla., 2004.

Ford, J. "Cross Cultural Conflict Resolution in Teams." 2001. http://www .mediate.com/articles/ford5.cfm.

Franish, B. (Producer), and Robinson, P. (Director). *Field of Dreams* [motion picture], Gordon Company, 1989.

Gerzon, M. *Leading Through Conflict: How Successful Leaders Transform Differences into Opportunities.* Boston: Harvard Business School Press, 2006.

Gibson, C., and Manuel, J. "Building Trust: Effective Multicultural Communication Processes in Virtual Teams." In C. Gibson and S. Cohen (eds.), *Virtual Teams That Work.* San Francisco: Jossey-Bass, 2003.

Goleman, D. *Emotional Intelligence.* New York: Bantam, 1995.

Goleman, D. *Destructive Emotions: How Can We Overcome Them?* New York: Bantam, 2003.

Goleman, D. *Social Intelligence.* New York: Bantam Books, 2007a.

Goleman, D. "Three Kinds of Empathy: Cognitive, Emotional, Compassionate." 2007b. http://www.danielgoleman.info/blog/2007/06/12/three-kinds-of-empathy-cognitive-emotional-compassionate/

Goleman, D., and Dass, R. *The Meditative Mind.* New York: HarperCollins, 1987.

Gratton, L., and Erickson, T. "Eight Ways to Build Collaborative Teams." *Harvard Business Review,* 2007, 85(11), 101–109.

Griffith, T., Mannix, E., and Neale, M. *"Conflict in Virtual Teams."* In C. Gibson and S. Cohen (eds.), *Virtual Teams That Work.* San Francisco: Jossey-Bass, 2003.

Gunaratana, B. *Mindfulness in Plain English.* Boston: Wisdom Publications, 2002.

Hambrick, D. "Corporate Coherence and the Top Management Team." In D. Hambrick, D. Nadler, and M. Tushman (eds.), *Navigating Change.* Boston: Harvard Business School Press, 1998.

Hammer, M. *Intercultural Conflict Style Inventory.* Ocean Pines, Md.: Hammer Consulting, 2003.

Hammer, M. "The Intercultural Style Inventory: A Conceptual Framework and Measure of Intercultural Conflict Resolution Approaches." *International Journal of Intercultural Relations,* 2005, 29, 675–695.

Harvard Negotiation Project. *The Hackerstar Negotiation.* New York: Morgan Guaranty Trust Company, 1985.

Hinds, P., and Bailey, D. "Out of Sight, Out of Sync: Understanding Conflict in Distributed Teams." *Organization Science,* 2003, 14(6), 615–632.

Homan, A., van Knippenberg, D., Van Kleef, G., and De Dreu, C. "Interacting Dimensions of Diversity: Cross Categorization and the Functioning of Diverse Work Groups." *Group Dynamics: Theory, Research, and Practice,* 2007a, 11(2), 79–94.

Homan, A., van Knippenberg, D., Van Kleef, G., and De Dreu, C. "Bridging Faultlines by Valuing Diversity: Diversity Beliefs, Information Evaluation, and Performance in Diverse Work Groups." *Journal of Applied Psychology,* 2007b, 92, 1189–1199.

Hotz, R. "How Your Brain Allows You to Walk in Another's Shoes." *Wall Street Journal,* Aug. 17, 2007, p. B1.

Jehn, K. "A Multimethod Examination of the Benefits and Detriments of Intragroup Conflict." *Administrative Science Quarterly,* 1995, 40, 256–282.

Jehn, K., Chadwick, C., and Thatcher, S. "To Agree or Not to Agree: The Effects of Value Congruence, Individual Demographic Dissimilarity, and Conflict on Workgroup Outcomes." *International Journal of Conflict Management,* 1997, 8(4), 287–305.

Jehn, K., and Chatman, J. "The Influence of Proportional and Perceptual Conflict Composition on Team Performance." *International Journal of Conflict Management,* 2000, 11(1), 56–73.

Jones, D. *Everyday Creativity.* Windsor, Calif.: Dewitt Jones Productions, 1999.

Jordan, P., and Troth, A. "Managing Emotions During Team Problem Solving: Emotional Intelligence and Conflict Resolution." *Human Performance*, 2004, *17*(2), 195–218.

Kankanhalli, A., Tan, B., and Wei, K. "Conflict and Performance in Global Virtual Teams." *Journal of Management Information Systems*, 2007, *23*(3), 237–274.

Katzenbach, J., and Smith, D. "The Discipline of Virtual Teams." *Leader to Leader*, Fall 2001, no. 22, 16–25.

Katzenbach, J., and Smith, D. *The Wisdom of Teams: Creating the High-Performance Organization*. New York: HarperCollins, 2003.

Kirton, M. *Adaption-Innovation in the Context of Diversity and Change.* London: Routledge, 2003.

Larson, C., and LaFasto, F. *Teamwork: What Must Go Right/What Can Go Wrong.* Thousand Oaks, Calif.: Sage, 1989.

Lencioni, P. *The Five Dysfunctions of a Team: A Leadership Fable.* San Francisco: Jossey-Bass, 2002.

Lencioni, P. *Overcoming the Five Dysfunctions of a Team: A Field Guide for Leaders, Managers, and Facilitators.* San Francisco: Jossey-Bass, 2005.

Lipnack, J., and Stamps, J. *Virtual Teams: Reaching Across Space, Time and Organizations with Technology.* Hoboken, N.J.: Wiley, 1997.

Lovelace, K., Shapiro, D., and Weingart, L. "Maximizing Cross-Functional New Product Teams' Innovativeness and Constraint Adherence: A Conflict Communications Perspective." *Academy of Management Journal*, 2001, *44*(4), 779–793.

Mayer, R., and Gavin, M. "Trust in Management and Performance: Who Minds the Shop While the Employees Watch the Boss?" *Academy of Management Journal*, 2005, *48*(5), 874–888.

McManigle, B. "CCL Poll: Conflict Competence." Leading Effectively, 2007. http://www.ccl.org/leadership/enewsletter/2007/AUGjulpollresults.aspx.

Miller, S. *Collaborative Team Skills.* Evergreen, Colo.: Interpersonal Communication Programs, 2007.

Montoya-Weiss, M., Mersey, A., and Sony, M. "Getting It Together: Temporal Coordination and Conflict Management in Global Virtual Teams." *Academy of Management Journal*, 2001, *44*(6), 1251–1262.

Mooney, A. "An Examination of Top Management Team Behavioral Integration as a Moderator of Functional Diversity and Firm Performance." Unpublished manuscript, July 2007.

Mooney, A., Holahan, P., and Amason, A. "Don't Take It Personally: Exploring Cognitive Conflict as a Mediator of Affective Conflict." *Journal of Management Science*, 2007, *44*(5), 733–758.

Mortensen, M., and Hinds, P. "Conflict and Shared Identity in Geographically Distributed Teams." *International Journal of Conflict Management*, 2001, *12*(3), 212–238.

Ochsner, K., Bunge, S., Gross, J., and Gabrieli, J. "Rethinking Feelings: An fMRI Study of the Cognitive Regulation of Emotion." *Journal of Cognitive Neuroscience*, 2002, *14*(8), 1215–1229.

Ochsner, K., and Gross, J. "The Cognitive Control of Emotion." *Trends in Cognitive Sciences*, 2005, *9*(5), 242–249.

Paul, S., Samarah, I., Seetharaman, P., and Mykytyn, P. "An Empirical Investigation of Collaborative Conflict Management Style in Group Support System-Based Global Virtual Teams." *Journal of Management Information Systems*, 2004–2005, *21*(3), 185–222.

Prati, L., and others. "Emotional Intelligence, Leadership Effectiveness, and Team Outcomes." *International Journal of Organizational Analysis*, 2003, *11*(1), 21–40.

Rahim, M., and Psenicka, C. "A Model of Emotional Intelligence and Conflict Management Strategies: A Study of Seven Countries." *International Journal of Organizational Analysis*, 2002, *10*(4), 302–326.

Rapisarda, B. "The Impact of Emotional Intelligence on Work Team Cohesiveness and Performance." *International Journal of Organizational Analysis*, 2002, *10*(4), 363–379.

Ray, R., and others. "Individual Differences in Trait Rumination and the Neural Systems Supporting Cognitive Reappraisal." *Cognitive, Affective and Behavioral Neuroscience*, 2005, *5*(2), 156–168.

Ringer, J. *Unlikely Teachers: Finding the Hidden Gifts in Daily Conflict.* Portsmouth, N.H.: OnePoint Press, 2006.

Roberto, M. *Why Great Leaders Don't Take Yes for an Answer.* Philadelphia: Wharton School Publishing, 2005.

Runde, C., and Flanagan, T. *Becoming a Conflict Competent Leader.* San Francisco: Jossey-Bass, 2007.

Schultz-Hardt, S., Jochims, M., and Frey, D. "Productive Conflict in Group Decision Making: Genuine and Contrived Dissent as Strategies to Counteract Biased Information Seeking." *Organizational Behavior and Human Decision Making*, 2002, *88*(2), 563–586.

Siegel, D. *The Mindful Brain: Reflection and Attunement in the Cultivation of Well-Being.* New York: Norton, 2007.

Simons, T., and Peterson, R. "Task and Relationship Conflict in Top Management Teams: The Pivotal Role of Intragroup Trust." *Journal of Applied Psychology*, 2000, *85*(1), 102–111.

Simsek, Z., Lubatkin, M., Veiga, J., and Dino, R. "Modeling the Multilevel Determinants of Top Management Team Behavioral Integration." *Academy of Management Journal*, 2005, *48*, 69–84.

Steil, L., and Bommelje, R. *Listening Leaders: The Ten Golden Rules to Listen, Lead and Succeed.* Minneapolis: Beaver's Pond Press, 2004.

Thomas, K., and Kilmann, R. *Thomas Kilmann Conflict Mode Instrument.* Mountain View, Calif.: Xicom, 1974.

Ting-Toomey, S., and Takai, J. "Explaining Intercultural Conflict: Promising Approaches and Directions." In J. Oetzel and S. Ting-Toomey (eds.), *The Sage Handbook of Conflict Communication: Integrating Theory, Research, and Practice.* Thousand Oaks, Calif.: Sage, 2006.

Tolle, E. *The Power of Now: A Guide to Spiritual Enlightenment.* Novato, Calif.: New World Library, 2004.

Tuckman, B. "Developmental Sequence in Small Groups." *Psychological Bulletin,* 1965, *63,* 384–395.

Ury, W. *The Third Side: Why We Fight and How We Can Stop.* New York: Penguin, 2000.

Ury, W. *The Power of a Positive No: How to Say No and Still Get to Yes.* New York: Bantam, 2007.

Von Glinow, M., Shapiro, D., and Brett, J. "Can We Talk, and Should We? Managing Emotional Conflict in Multicultural Teams." *Academy of Management Review,* 2004, *29*(4), 578–592.

Wheelan, S. *Creating Effective Teams: A Guide for Members and Leaders.* Thousand Oaks, Calif.: Sage, 2005.

Wilmot, W., and Hocker, J. *Interpersonal Conflict.* (6th ed.) New York: McGraw-Hill, 2001.

Yeatts, D., and Hyten, C. *High-Performing Self-Managed Work Teams: A Comparison of Theory to Practice.* Thousand Oaks, Calif.: Sage, 1998.

Zaccaro, S., and Bader, P. "E-Leadership and the Challenges of Leading E-Teams: Minimizing the Bad and Maximizing the Good." *Organizational Dynamics,* 2003, *31*(4), 377–387.

# The Authors

**Craig E. Runde,** director of new program development at the Eckerd College Leadership Development Institute (LDI), oversees training and development on the Conflict Dynamics Profile assessment instrument. He is the coauthor of *Becoming a Conflict Competent Leader* (Jossey-Bass, 2007) and is a frequent speaker and commentator on workplace conflict issues. Before joining LDI, he was the director of the International Center for Computer Enhanced Learning at Wake Forest University. He received his B.A. from Harvard University, M.L.L. from the University of Denver, and J.D. from Duke University. He has practiced law in Colorado and has taught at the University of Minnesota Law School and Wake Forest University.

**Tim A. Flanagan,** director of custom programs for LDI, earned his M.A. at the Ohio State University and worked in higher education for eight years before entering the human resource development field in 1985. His experience includes leading the senior leadership development programs at the Harris Corporation; managing consulting services for Development Dimensions International; building the training program at AAA, Tampa; and guiding the custom development of discovery learning programs at Paradigm Learning. He is a frequent presenter at professional conferences and has consulted with scores of leading national and international firms. He is the coauthor of *Becoming a Conflict Competent Leader* (Jossey-Bass, 2007).

# Index

# About the Center for Creative Leadership

The Center for Creative Leadership (CCL) is a nonprofit, educational institution with international reach. Since the Center's founding in 1970, its mission has been to advance the understanding, practice, and development of leadership for the benefit of society worldwide.

Devoted to leadership education and research, CCL works annually with more than two thousand organizations and twenty thousand individuals from the private, public, education, and nonprofit sectors. The Center's five campuses span three continents: Greensboro, North Carolina; Colorado Springs, Colorado; and San Diego, California, in North America; Brussels, Belgium, in Europe; and Singapore in Asia. In addition, sixteen Network Associates around the world offer selected CCL programs and assessments.

CCL draws strength from its nonprofit status and educational mission, which provide unusual flexibility in a world where quarterly profits often drive thinking and direction. It has the freedom to be objective, wary of short-term trends, and motivated foremost by its mission—hence our substantial and sustained investment in leadership research. Although CCL's work is always grounded in a strong foundation of research, it focuses on achieving a beneficial impact in the real world. Its efforts are geared to be practical and action oriented, helping leaders and their organizations more effectively achieve their goals and vision. The desire to transform learning and ideas into action provides the impetus for CCL's programs, assessments, publications, and services.

## Capabilities

CCL's activities encompass leadership education, knowledge generation and dissemination, and building a community centered on leadership. CCL is broadly recognized for excellence in executive education, leadership development, and innovation by sources such as *BusinessWeek*, the *Financial Times*, the *New York Times*, and the *Wall Street Journal*.

## Open-Enrollment Programs

Fourteen open-enrollment courses are designed for leaders at all levels, as well as people responsible for leadership development and training at their organizations. This portfolio offers distinct choices for participants seeking a particular learning environment or type of experience. Some programs are structured specifically around small group activities, discussion, and personal reflection, while others offer hands-on opportunities through business simulations, artistic exploration, team-building exercises, and new-skills practice. Many of these programs offer private one-on-one sessions with a feedback coach.

For a complete listing of programs, visit http://www.ccl.org/programs.

## Customized Programs

CCL develops tailored educational solutions for more than one hundred client organizations around the world each year. Through this applied practice, CCL structures and delivers programs focused on specific leadership development needs within the context of defined organizational challenges, including innovation, the merging of cultures, and the development of a broader pool of leaders. The objective is to help organizations develop, within their own cultures, the leadership capacity they need to address challenges as they emerge.

Program details are available at http://www.ccl.org/custom.

## Coaching

CCL's suite of coaching services is designed to help leaders maintain a sustained focus and generate increased momentum toward achieving their goals. These coaching alternatives vary in depth and duration and serve a variety of needs, from helping an executive sort through career and life issues to working with an organization to integrate coaching into its internal development process. Our coaching offerings, which can supplement program attendance or be customized for specific individual or team needs, are based on our ACS model of assessment, challenge, and support.

Learn more about CCL's coaching services at http://www.ccl.org/coaching.

## Assessment and Development Resources

CCL pioneered 360-degree feedback and believes that assessment provides a solid foundation for learning, growth, and transformation and that development truly happens when an individual recognizes the need to change. CCL offers a broad selection of assessment tools, online resources, and simulations that can help individuals, teams, and organizations increase their self-awareness, facilitate their own learning, enable their development, and enhance their effectiveness.

CCL's assessments are profiled at http://www.ccl.org/assessments.

## Publications

The theoretical foundation for many of our programs, as well as the results of CCL's extensive and often groundbreaking research, can be found in the scores of publications issued by CCL Press and through the Center's alliance with Jossey-Bass, a Wiley imprint. Among these are landmark works, such as *Breaking the Glass Ceiling*, *The Lessons of Experience*, and *The Center for Creative Leadership Handbook of Leadership Development*, as well as quick-read guidebooks focused on core aspects of leadership.

CCL publications provide insights and practical advice to help individuals become more effective leaders, develop leadership training within organizations, address issues of change and diversity, and build the systems and strategies that advance leadership collectively at the institutional level.

A complete listing of CCL publications is available at http://www.ccl.org/publications.

## Leadership Community

To ensure that the Center's work remains focused, relevant, and important to the individuals and organizations it serves, CCL maintains a host of networks, councils, and learning and virtual communities that bring together alumni, donors, faculty, practicing leaders, and thought leaders from around the globe. CCL also forges relationships and alliances with individuals, organizations, and associations that share its values and mission. The energy, insights, and support from these relationships help shape and sustain CCL's educational and research practices and provide its clients with an added measure of motivation and inspiration as they continue their lifelong commitment to leadership and learning.

To learn more, visit http://www.ccl.org/connected.

## Research

CCL's portfolio of programs, products, and services is built on a solid foundation of behavioral science research. The role of research at CCL is to advance the understanding of leadership and to transform learning into practical tools for participants and clients. CCL's research is the hub of a cycle that transforms knowledge into applications and applications into knowledge, thereby illuminating the way organizations think about and enact leadership and leader development.

Find out more about current research initiatives at http://www.ccl.org/research.

For additional information about CCL, please visit http://www.ccl.org or call Client Services at 336-545-2810.